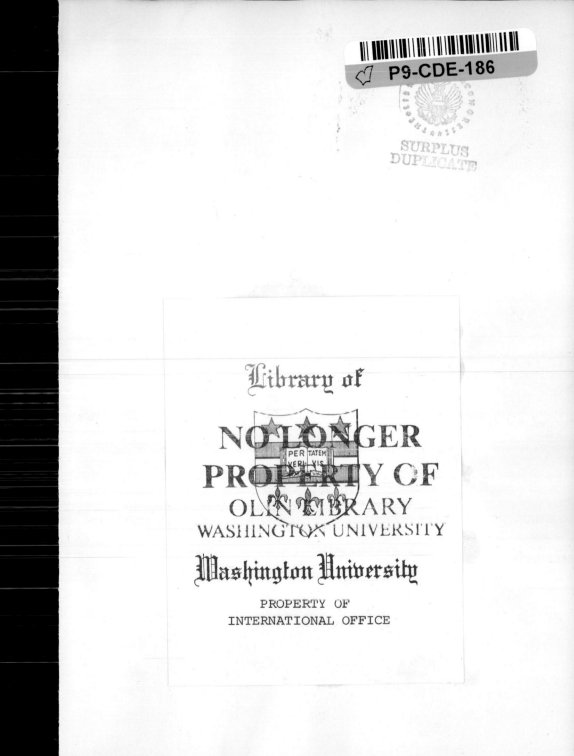

CHINA

The People's Middle Kingdom and the U. S. A.

JOHN K. FAIRBANK

THE BELKNAP PRESS OF
HARVARD UNIVERSITY PRESS

CAMBRIDGE, MASSACHUSETTS · 1967

For Wilma

PREFACE: THE USES

OF CHINA SPECIALISTS

Area specialists by definition try to stand between cultures, interpreting one to another. For their academic livelihood they usually teach history; but it is the history of a foreign people and culture, and they teach it to their American students. They go further and tell their fellow citizens about it in speech and writing. When the area is a big public problem like China, the specialist may soon become a pundit and dispense instant wisdom like a columnist. This in itself says something about the American scene in the 1960s.

The fact is that the China specialist, a recognizable though transitory species, has been called into being by public need. China is so big and so different that it does no good to echo Rex Harrison's plaint in *My Fair Lady*, "Why can't *they* be more like *us?*" We have to accept and face the fact that the Chinese quarter of mankind live on the other side of a cultural gap, and our effort to bridge this gap in the next decade may make us or break us.

Thus the first characteristic of a China specialist is that he feels he has an urgent message for his fellow men, as a sort of missionary in reverse. Such people, of course, ought to be watched. Where would they lead us? Why? Suspicion easily attaches to them.

As professional scholars, China specialists in my observation usually have a lively sense of their own inadequacies. Yet as latter-day missionaries *manqués*, with a vision of conditions and trends on the other side of the gap, they feel they have a contribution to make. In response to public demand they usually succeed in overcoming their modesty. In the end their success in depicting the cultural gap is measured by whether they are attacked from only one side or (preferably) from both sides.

Yet China specialists, though they try to be men in between, inevitably are one-sided. In basic attitudes they reflect their own culture and its predispositions, and one can therefore question both the adequacy of their grasp of China and also the degree of their understanding of America. In short, to deal with Sino-American relations we need to know both sides profoundly well. Both are bodies in motion, moving very fast. History alone cannot give us a complete picture, much less a future projection. It follows that China specialists in their assumptions and analyses are likely to mirror our American culture-bound blind spots. In these essays, for example, I have attached a fundamental value to our traditional institutions of the supremacy of law, the rights of the individual, and the self-determination of peoples. Yet I cannot foresee their triumph in China. Will they bring us into conflict there?

Unfortunately, the sincerity of our beliefs does not ensure their worldwide triumph. We should recall how the Japanese had China specialists before World War II, including able scholars and sincere patriots. They seldom questioned Japan's imperial way, and they tended to underestimate Chinese nationalism. They looked at Kuomintang China but saw the Ch'ing dynasty and the warlords.

The essays in this volume also have an obvious historical bias. They say little about China's new economy, the application of Maoism to local government, and other portentous changes of today. Perhaps their historical hindsight merely tells us what we should have done in 1900.

In short, the reader faces two major pitfalls. The first is that historical knowledge, as a picture of the present, is always partly out of date. Revolutions create discontinuity. Who can tell the actual degree of carryover from China's great tradition to Mao Tse-tung's great revolution? We may assume too much from what we know of the past and know too little of what is happening this moment. The second pitfall is that we still discuss "China" as a single entity, as Chinese patriots also do, even though this "China" embraces a whole subcontinent of perhaps 750 million people. How can this not be an oversimplification?

The solution is to make every citizen become his own China pundit. "Experts" can still be useful, but only on special aspects of the problem. The Chinese-American confrontation is a major issue of public policy. It cannot be left to the old-style Sinologues, who used to explain China-in-general, nor even to the new-style Sinologists, who use Chinese for specialized research. China's different ways, as a distinctly separate society and culture, are no longer exotica on a far horizon; they are realities on our doorstep.

Both the difficulties and the fascination of China punditry are illustrated by the Red Guards who surfaced in Peking in mid-August 1966. They were described as youthful vigilante gangs rampaging through the streets, harassing "enemies" of Mao's thought, ransacking people's homes, humiliating their elders, lecturing their teachers, changing old street names, demolishing old monuments, and generally carrying on like teenage delinquents massively organized by a Chinese Joseph McCarthy. Soon Chairman Mao was wearing the Red Guards' armband and reviewing them one or two million at a time as successive waves gathered in Peking and dispersed to the provinces. Soviet and Chinese Nationalist propagandists mounted campaigns to play up this Maoist excess and violence, which made it no easier to get at the facts. At the same time, the Peking politburo was reshuffled and General Lin Piao, fresh from his success in fostering Maoism in the army, emerged as the Chairman's presumptive heir. What was this all about? It was a great chance for instant insight and several lines of analysis were at once available.

First, one must view the Red Guards in Chairman Mao's own perspective. At seventy-two he was known to feel concern lest the fires of revolution burn out: how could youth experience the iconoclastic fanaticism of revolution and be blooded in the cause, except by being called to violent action? The "great proletarian cultural revolution," under way for many months but now given a new push by the Red Guards, was against the "four olds"—old ideas, old habits, old customs, old culture—to which was added for completeness everything foreign. Together, the past and the outside world indubitably had created China's problems and so deserved attack. For the young students in the Red Guards, this campaign was meant to be a rerun of the original struggle for "liberation," a way of revitalizing China's "permanent revolution." Critics asked, what real problems would it solve? Was not Mao, with his will-conquers-all formulas for getting China out of her quagmire, a bit too nostalgic for the simplicities of the years of hope at Yenan, when his leadership was creating a new state power and the really insoluble problems still lay ahead?

A second line of analysis stemmed from Mao's many recent setbacks—the economic chaos created by his utopian Great Leap Forward of 1958, the widening Sino-Soviet split since 1960, the slowdown in industrialization, the precariousness of China's food supply in the face of the population deluge. To these central concerns were added the setbacks abroad—in the Afro-Asian bloc, on the Indian border, in Indonesia, and also in Vietnam where the Maoist "people's war of liberation" was no longer winning. All this suggested that Chairman Mao was on the defensive, facing a considerable opposition within his party. In this context the Red Guards appeared as an irregular, extra-party device, engineered by Mao to pressure his critics. With support from Lin and the army, the Chairman could bypass the Young Communist League, mobilize youth in this new red crusade, and attack as "demons and monsters" the disenchanted party members among his erstwhile supporters.

The revolution had always operated through campaigns like this one, directing overwhelming public pressure against one or another class element that had to be "struggled with" and refashioned or eliminated. But to mount a campaign from outside the Communist Party of China, the bearer of the revolutionary mission and origin of Mao's power, against high-ranking members and whole units of the party apparatus was surely a new and desperate move. The opposition to Mao seemed, by inference, very strong.

Finally the distant observer versed in the broad outlines of Chinese history may try to put this struggle among the Peking leadership into a longer perspective. Can any régime really ever solve China's problems? The Chinese people's dual heritage of pride and poverty suggests perhaps not.

If China's leaders could be content with second-best status their people could share an austere living standard and a rich culture while modernization gradually spread through the economy with the slow accumulation of skills and capital. But Chinese leaders, depending so much upon their own prestige, have to be more face-conscious than most rulers, and as patriots they are in a hurry to see China catch up with the great powers. Moreover, they are committed at the very least, to the centralized government of what will soon be a billion persons—a polity on a scale the world has never seen before. One cannot help wondering if the sense of China's grandeur and the urge for unity do not create infeasible political goals, infeasible in the sense that the economic cost of realizing them is inordinately high?

Mao's course has been explicitly guided by politics more than by economics. The Great Leap and the anti-Soviet polemic have both proved counterproductive. In recent months the universities have been closed, though the skills they produce are essential for economic growth. In short, to put "politics in command" and be more "red" than "expert" is no way to develop an economy.

A historian will note that Chinese bureaucrats from early times were great admonishers and manipulators of the common people, trained to elaborate the administrative mechanism, supervise its operation, keep an intuitive eye out for popular discontent, sit atop the body politic and keep it in order, but never to foster economic growth as the main aim of the state. Times have changed, and industrialization is China's modern aim. But has the style of government, its instincts and habits, changed sufficiently? Chairman Mao and many others seem to think not. Yet here is where Mao gets into his particular quagmire, for he wants to break out of China's tradition and change her condition, but pride leads him into doing it with a great stress on independence and self-sufficiency, relying only on China's own capacities, which are perhaps inadequate.

All this has implications for our China policy. Some of these are pursued in the essays that follow. First published as articles, they have been slightly updated and edited to avoid repetition.

J.K.F.

Cambridge, Massachusetts
November 1966

CONTENTS

PART I

CHINA'S REVOLUTION IN

THE LIGHT OF HER PAST

1 A NATION IMPRISONED

BY HER HISTORY

A curious contradiction haunts Chairman Mao's revolution: the more he seeks to make China new, the more he seems to fall back on old Chinese ways of doing it. Two thirds of a century ago, in the midsummer madness of 1900, the Boxer bands who were officially commissioned to exterminate foreigners in North China were composed largely of peasant youth and they pursued their ends with the same zeal displayed today by Chairman Mao's officially commissioned "Red Guards" in their attack on all things foreign. But where the Boxers wanted to do away merely with Western influence in China, the Red Guards express a double frustration: they also want to wipe out China's "old ideas, old customs, old habits, old culture."

Chairman Mao is struggling not only against Western influence but also against the hold of China's ancient past. First, he is trying to revolutionize the world's biggest political unit. No one has ever before even tried to govern 700 million people through a single unitary regime, let alone remake their whole way of life and thought. But this is not all. In the second place, China happens to be the oldest political unit with a continuous tradition. Chinese history

From *Life*, September 23, 1966.

3

lists twenty-five dynasties. Where Mao stands today on the Gate of Heavenly Peace facing Red Square in Peking, dozens of emperors, Sons of Heaven, ruled for hundreds of years, building up the monumental inertia of Chinese tradition. When Mao wants to strike down this tradition, he can find only methods used before. China's long history has him in quicksand—as he struggles, he becomes more immersed in the attitudes and dreams inherited from China's past.

The reader may be warned that this is an historian's view. But I think the great influence of history on events in China will be plain enough to anyone who looks into it.

To start with, there is the fact, elementary but central, that for more than four thousand years the Chinese have lived in the same area. While the center of Western civilization moved from the eastern Mediterranean through Greece and Rome, across France and England and out over the Atlantic, the Chinese stayed at home in East Asia— isolated, walled in by mountains and deserts to the west, jungle to the south, steppe and tundra on the north, and boundless ocean on the east. The same mountain ranges and river flood plains that shaped their long history are still around them today. Try to imagine all of our Western past having occurred within the present United States and you will get a faint idea of China's self-centered experience down to a century ago. It is as though we could go and see the Egyptian pyramids along the Mississippi above Cairo, Illinois, or could have the Acropolis lit up every night on Capitol Hill in Washington, or had excavated the Roman Forum in downtown Philadelphia and marked the site of Magna Carta in a field between Lexington and Concord.

Within these natural confines the Chinese way of life gradually expanded, from the Yellow River to the Yangtze Valley and on across South China. While Westerners became seafarers, colonizing distant shores of the Mediterranean and Atlantic, the Chinese remained farmers and administrators in their continental empire. Their development was inward rather than outward, and stressed the social order more than the individual. Staying at home, they so well perfected their own sociopolitical order that by about 1000 A.D. they led the world in the art of government.

The geographical separateness of China was reinforced by the growth of a series of distinctive institutions, beginning with her ideographic writing system. The strength of this kind of writing lies in its being understandable as symbols of meaning, as numerals are understood, rather than as symbols of sound, as alphabetic writing is understood. Thus, as Chinese writing spread out from North China, it could be learned and used in the Shanghai, Foochow, Amoy, and Canton areas of South China and in Vietnam, Korea, and Japan, even though the dialects or languages these people spoke were quite different from that of North China. The Chinese characters gave them a common bond of classical learning and made for cultural and political unity within a subcontinent far larger than Europe.

China's unity was achieved early and, when broken—almost in a cycle of unity-disunity-unity—always revived. With no outlet in seafaring, the scores of small city-states that grew up on the North China plain competed instead in war and politics. By the sixth century B.C. about ten big states had absorbed all the rest, and in the great unification of 221 B.C. the Warring States were finally conquered by the state of Ch'in, from which came the Western name, China. The administrators of the Han dynasty (202 B.C.–220 A.D.) consolidated the centralized empire. The ideological cement they used was Confucianism.

Confucius lived around 500 B.C., a philosopher-adviser to the rulers of his time on matters of statecraft and how to achieve, and then maintain, power and political stability. As it finally developed, Imperial Confucianism added a good deal of Realpolitik to the original teachings of the sage, although the gap between founder and institution was hardly as great as that between, say, Jesus of Nazareth and the medieval Papacy. Confucianism gave the Chinese despot ethical respectability. It supplied the central myth of the Chinese state, the political fiction of rule by virtue.

Even so, this Chinese political theory was a good deal more rational than the European theory of the divine right of kings. First, the cycles of nature and of life—the lunar month, the solar year, planting and harvesting, birth and death—all demonstrate that the human social order is part of the order of nature. The Son of Heaven was viewed as functioning where they met, at the very top of the human scene, and kept man and nature in harmony. The emperor conducted the cosmic rituals at the altar of heaven or atop the sacred mountains. He set the calendar. He took personal responsibility for drought, flood, and other acts of nature, as though his own virtue had been at fault.

Second, he set the moral example for all men—and this was felt to be the real secret of his power. His supremely virtuous conduct moved all civilized mankind to awe and obedience. "When a prince's personal conduct is correct," Confucius said in the *Analects,* "his government is effective without the issuing of orders. If his personal conduct is not correct, he may issue orders but they will not be followed." Chinese power holders ever since, down through Chiang Kai-shek and Mao Tse-tung, have claimed a moral leadership. Even if they lacked it in fact, they have still preserved it in the record. But when such a paragon loses power, sure enough, the record will later show that he had already lost his moral stature.

In this system, a ruler's policies were an inseparable part

of his virtuous conduct. To criticize his policies was to undermine his prestige (or face) and therefore his power. The Western idea of a "loyal opposition," which could criticize a policy while still expecting the policy maker to stay in office, never took root in China.

Many political inventions buttressed the strong monarchy. The examination system, for example, opened official careers to the talented and ambitious some thirteen centuries before we got around to civil service examinations in the West. For century after century the Chinese examinees indoctrinated themselves in state orthodoxy by memorizing the official commentaries on the Confucian classics. A successful candidate spent ten or fifteen years' hard work at this task. Not surprisingly, he seldom thereafter produced a novel or rebellious idea. Yet he had put himself through this intellectual wringer by his own choice and at his own expense. It was a neat device.

Equally neat and useful was the legal system of mutual or collective responsibility: all family members were responsible for one another, and all neighbors were responsible for neighboring households. If your brother did wrong and absconded, *you* would pay. So you kept an eye on him. In the result, everybody watched everybody— again at no cost to the state. This ancient invention lies behind the networks of informers that operate in China (and on Taiwan) today.

Innumerable other administrative devices and self-balancing institutions helped to keep society in order. All were the handiwork of the scholar-official ruling class who were the inheritors of the art of statecraft and supervised the activities of peasants, merchants, and artisans. Indissolubly wedded to Confucian principles, dependent on the imperial patronage, the mandarins became the world's most formidable establishment, highly conservative in outlook, highly skilled in manipulating people.

7

Toward surrounding states, including Turkic and Mongol tribes from the Inner Asian grasslands whose powerful cavalry sometimes broke in through the Great Wall, the Chinese developed not what we think of as normal foreign relations but the institution of tribute. Though the "outer barbarians" were only on the fringe of the Chinese world order, the awe-inspiring example of the emperor made them acknowledge him as the center of civilization. "He nourished them like their father and mother," wrote a Chinese enthusiast in 1839. "He gave them illumination like the sun and moon. When they were starving, he fed them. . . . When they came to him, he took them to his bosom." And, it might be added, when they brought tribute and kowtowed—three kneelings and nine prostrations—at Peking, the emperor's gifts to them made it well worth their while. In short, when China was strong militarily, the barbarians' tribute could be exacted. When China was weak militarily, she was still strong economically, and the barbarians' tribute could be bought and paid for. Either way, the ceremonies of tribute and the emperor's prestige were preserved.

The final achievement of the mandarins was the capacity they developed to let non-Chinese conquerors—the Mongols (1279–1368) or especially the Manchus (1644–1911)—come in and rule China as emperors at Peking while the empire went on being governed through a Chinese bureaucracy in the old familiar Chinese way. This assimilation of alien dynastic rule, sometimes oversimplified as "China absorbing her conquerors," tended to emphasize the universal, nonnational character of the monarchy. The alien emperors stressed Confucian culturalism and so held back the growth of Chinese nationalism.

Not all these political devices were unique to China, nor did they always function well. The Chinese polity had its share of corruption, intrigue, greed, and dirty work. But the total effect was to give China the world's most stable, skilled, and sophisticated government by the time the Dark Ages were engulfing Europe. Westerners who managed to reach China could well be amazed at the enormous size and stability of the Chinese state. In the thirteenth century, Marco Polo noted that in the scenic old capital of Hang-chow, one of the world's great cities, "persons who inhabit the same street, both men and women, from the mere circumstances of neighborhood, appear like one family." As late as the seventeenth and eighteenth centuries, during the sixty-year reigns of the great K'ang Hsi and Ch'ien Lung emperors, Jesuit missionaries at Peking could hold up China's material peace and prosperity as a model for Europe to aim at. On this point the rulers of China agreed with them. When England sought diplomatic contact in 1793, Ch'ien Lung wrote a famous edict to King George III: "The virtue and prestige of the Celestial Dynasty having spread far and wide, the kings of the myriad nations come by land and sea with all sorts of precious things. Consequently there is nothing we lack. . . . We have never set much store on strange or ingenious objects, nor do we need any more of your country's manufactures."

Yet this Chinese self-image of sufficiency and condescending superiority masked the fact that China's development had fallen behind that of Europe. The ambitious, quarrelsome Europeans, off on the small westernmost peninsulas and islands of the great Eurasian land mass, had been developing the dynamism of modern life, evidenced in forms of growth and violent expansion that we tag for convenience as nationalism, individualism, Christian missions, science, capitalism, industrialism, and so on. By the end of the eighteenth century the Europeans had already overrun much of the earth. But the Chinese, in their own ample corner of the world, had remained contentedly unaware of their inadequacies and of the potential danger to them in these new developments. As George III's envoy, the Earl of Macartney, noted in his journal, "The Empire of China is an old, crazy, first-rate Man of War. . . . She may, perhaps, not sink outright; she may drift some time as a wreck, and will then be dashed to pieces on the shore; but she can never be rebuilt on the old bottom."

In the early nineteenth century, China was suffering from a great population explosion. One symptom of her weakness and demoralization was the growth of opium smoking. Far from being an old Chinese custom, this vice had been practically unknown in China before 1800, just as it is all but unknown today. Yet the nineteenth century saw it become widespread, stimulated and supplied by opium imports from India sold by British merchants to the Chinese distributors. To suppress the opium traffic China's rulers tried to coerce the British within the framework of the outworn tribute system. But the British seized the opportunity to attack China's whole posture of isolation and superiority. In fighting the Opium War of 1840–1842, they felt themselves the righteous champions of modern (Western) civilization against China's backwardness.

In a general way, this war set a pattern that still applies to our relations with China, for the British were demanding that China join the international order according to Western rules. In the 1840s the demand, to which the Manchu emperors were ultimately obliged to accede, was for free trade (1) in a free market without official monopolies, (2) to be taxed by a regularly enforced published tariff, (3) at ports where foreigners would enjoy the protection of Western law administered by foreign consuls functioning on Chinese soil. These privileges—plus the right to seek Christian converts—were gained by the unequal treaties that remained in force for a full century from 1842 to 1943. Meanwhile the opium trade, though still prohibited by the Emperor at Peking, was left for him to prevent as best he could. When this proved impossible, it grew in volume and value, and was made legal after 1858, creating more addicts and further corrupting Chinese life.

By and large, however, China remained self-concerned and unresponsive to this new barbarian invasion from the West. Until 1860 the Westerners were kept to the southeast coast, where the early missionaries made few converts. When violent domestic rebellions after 1850 mobilized Chinese peasants against the Manchu-Chinese ruling class, the dynasty at Peking saw the rebels, with their strong anti-Confucian bent, as a more basic threat to the traditional way of life than the commercial-minded foreigners were. Western help was even accepted in suppressing the most important of these movements, the Taiping Rebellion. Although this made sense to the Confucian minded ruling class of the 1860s, it is, of course, denounced in retrospect by Chinese patriots of today.

But time was not on the side of Confucianism. The foreign encroachment continued inexorably. Within two generations, the once great ancient center of civilization had become a semicolony of smaller foreign countries. What had happened?

China's rulers could hardly comprehend the rising flood that was slowly engulfing them. In the 1860s, while reasserting the tried and true principles of Imperial Confucian government, they went out and bought Western arms and gunboats. Yet even this was done over conservative objections: "The fundamental effort lies in the minds of people, not in techniques . . . why is it necessary to learn from the barbarians?" In the 1870s and 1880s leading officials began movements for Western-type industrialization and governmental reform. Justification for this was culled from the classics but the classical examination system, which provided the base for the established order, was left unchanged. It was all too little, too late. The old Chinese state-and-society could not be jacked up and modernized. Instead, the whole structure had to be torn down.

Like all historical accounts, the above is, of course, an interpretation. Many Chinese patriots of today prefer to stress, instead of China's weakness, the foreigners' aggressiveness. Like Chairman Mao, they are tempted to ascribe the old China's downfall to the monstrous evils of imperialism, including in this catchall not only foreign trade, wars of aggression, and economic exploitation by the imperialist powers, but also the "cultural imperialism" of the missionary movement. Obviously, a great deal hinges on how one interprets the decline of the Chinese Empire in the nineteenth century.

I would not underrate the avarice, enterprise, and self-righteous aggressiveness of our Victorian ancestors of the age of imperialism. I merely doubt that they were able to break down the Chinese Empire all alone. They tried, of course. Western merchants did seek a fast buck, and Western missionaries looking for "heathen" converts did indeed undermine Confucianism and begin China's modernization in many ways. But the real key was the *quality* of China's response to Western contact. The foreigners acted mainly as catalysts. In Japan in the same period, foreigners set up the same system of privilege by treaty and found that patriotic samurai, when they were angered, had a tendency to draw their long swords and cut foreigners in two rather than acquiesce. In Japan, loyalty to feudal leaders could—and did—develop quickly into nationalism,

much as it had in Europe. But the Chinese loyalty was not
to leaders but to their ancient culture and institutions.
And when these proved inadequate for modern life, their
loyalty was left without a focus. Japan westernized with
amazing speed. China fell apart.

I think most historians would agree that the Chinese in
the nineteenth century were undone by the very factors
that had given them such early success in the art of government. Over the centuries they had solved one problem
of stability after another, but always within the framework
of East Asia. When the West broke in from outside and
presented new problems, the old solutions were produced
and tried again but they would not work. For example, the
Chinese ruling class of the seventeenth century was com-
pelled to let the Manchu barbarians move into the power
structure as emperors at the very top. Nevertheless, Imperial Confucianism subsequently achieved new heights.
In much the same way, the Manchu-Chinese ruling class of
the mid-nineteenth century was ready to let the powerful
British barbarians participate in the power structure of the
empire, and after 1860 many British administrators did indeed become Chinese civil servants under the emperor.
But the British, unlike the Manchus, did not try to learn
and perpetuate the Chinese way. They represented a different scheme of things entirely, and their presence only
helped to undermine the Chinese system.

Little in the Chinese model was suited to the dynamism
of modern Europe. In a world just entering the heyday of
nationalism, the Manchu rulers, being non-Chinese, had to
soft-pedal it. In a world just undergoing the Industrial
Revolution, China—for all her earlier achievements in science and inventions like printing and gunpowder—had
little innate interest in scientific technology or the substitution of steam machinery for muscle power in transport and

13

manufacture. Again, in an era when mass literacy, the press, democracy, and representative government were fueling the aggressiveness of Western nations, the great peasant mass of China remained politically inert. The small elite continued to monopolize literacy and learning, politics, and power. It was still as the classics said: "Some men labor with their minds and govern others; some labor with their hands and are governed by others."

The very writing system also served to slow down the assimilation of foreign ideas. The Japanese, the Koreans, and the Vietnamese had all developed phonetic systems of writing to supplement their use of Chinese characters. They could thus import foreign words by sound as new additions to the language. But Chinese was still written only in ideographic characters. Foreign words like "radio" could not easily be taken in by imitating their sound but only by using characters to express their meaning. Since traditional meanings were already attached to all the characters, ambiguity could result and Chinese readers could cling to the old rather than the new meanings. Moreover, the kind of language reform that Europe had achieved in the Renaissance—the writing down of language as it was spoken in the vernacular—was not pushed until 1917. The ideographic characters themselves, unchanged since the time of the First Emperor, have only recently been simplified and are still an obstacle to rapid literacy.

Finally, the Chinese were stuck with their proud traditions and their inborn conviction of superiority. They had never thought of themselves as borrowing culture from outer barbarians or acknowledging their cultural equality. The Chinese could not now accept the idea that they themselves were a cultural minority, out of step with the world at large.

14

How far the times were out of joint can be gauged by the frustrations of China's chief modernizer in the late nineteenth century, Li Hung-chang. This outstanding bureaucrat rose to power as commander of a new army whose foreign guns he paid for with trade revenues from the rising port of Shanghai. During four decades he tried everything—building arsenals and steamships, opening mines and railways, developing a navy, trying to pacify the French on the Indochina border and to keep the Russians and Japanese out of Korea. Until the new Japanese fleet sank much of the new Chinese fleet in 1894, in one of the first modern naval battles, Li remained the big official of the day. But consider his difficulties—he had to keep the favor of the Manchu ruler at Peking, the empress dowager, whose penchant for court amenities led her to set up a widespread system of corruption. Her officials even diverted funds from the navy to rebuild her summer palace. The establishment often torpedoed Li's projects, and he himself played the game of corruption. When the Japanese negotiator of 1895, Itō Hirobumi, asked him, "Why is it that up to now not a single thing has been changed or reformed?" Li Hung-chang could only reply, "Affairs in my country have been so confined by tradition. . . . I am ashamed of having excessive wishes and lacking the power to fulfill them." He lived just long enough to negotiate the protocol that ended the Boxer incident but mortgaged China's revenues to the foreign powers.

Looking back over China's experience as an out-of-date civilization coming late and awkwardly, like a mastodon left over from a bygone age, into the rapidly changing modern world, one can begin to appreciate the modern task of metamorphosis. One of the great leaders, Liang Ch'i-ch'ao, wrote in 1922, "China during the last fifty years has been like a silkworm becoming a moth, or a snake removing its skin. These are naturally very difficult and painful processes."

The effort to modernize was aided by foreigners who swarmed over the prostrate empire after 1900, but their helpfulness was often humiliating to the new Chinese nationalists. Meantime the old empress dowager, intent on preserving the Manchu power, could find no way to modernize China without fostering revolutionaries and digging the dynasty's grave. By the time the collapse came in 1911, three years after her death, the structure of Imperial Confucianism was already rotted out. The end of the examination system in 1905 had broken the educational monopoly of the classics. Overthrow of the Manchu dynasty in 1911 also threw out the Son of Heaven as an institution. A government which for more than two thousand years had centered on the monarchy now had no monarch. As Mongolia and Tibet broke away from the Chinese Republic, the empire disintegrated. The Chinese people, so long accustomed to the central authority of the Son of Heaven, now confronted their time of greatest change without a leader.

2 AN AMERICAN VIEW OF CHINA'S MODERNIZATION

The modern supranational world chiefly lacks the presence of China, which is the country least integrated in the modern international scene, just as it is the most distinctively different of all the great world societies. The comparative underdevelopment of China includes the underdevelopment of Chinese historical studies both at home and abroad, and this has left the world with very diverse images of the origins and processes of modern history there. Consequently, the potentialities and trends of the future are more obscure and diverse in the minds of the various peoples. In the nineteenth century the traditional Confucian self-image in China was gradually destroyed; yet the Marxist-Leninist image that has taken its place, for the moment at least, does not seem to fit the Chinese scene very well. It is also at variance with the general trend of modern historical understanding in the international

From *Bulletin,* International House of Japan, October 1964; an address to a Japanese audience.

17

world. For this reason, it seems to me particularly necessary to try to create in our minds a common image of what has happened in modern China in recent times—a picture of Chinese modernization.

Understanding the modern historical development of China is important because if the United States and Japan, for example, have widely different images of it, they may draw very different conclusions as to future potentialities. In general, I assume that our common image of modernization must draw upon the social sciences for their basic patterns of interpretation. Let us deal first with the international framework in which Chinese modernization has been occurring; second, with certain persistent features of the traditional order both in institutions and in ideology; and third, with the growth of a modern order in China in which the present regime is the current phase.

The international framework of Chinese modern history is usually characterized by the term "imperialism," which seems to connote, in this case, a broad across-the-board conflict between states and societies and even cultures and civilizations. On this point, I am inclined to agree with both Chiang Kai-shek and Mao Tse-tung. The Western expansion of the nineteenth century, so commonly characterized by its victims as imperialism, was a great deal more than the political domination which that word usually has connoted in Western history. The Western expansion also involved a good deal more than the economic influence which is particularly stressed in Leninism. It involved, in short, a conflict of cultures on a broader scale.

The Western expansion of the nineteenth century went through two well-marked phases, in the first of which the Western powers set up systems of unequal treaties as a basis for trade and evangelism. Thus, in the decades before 1880, unequal-treaty systems were established in China beginning in 1842, in Japan from 1854, in Siam from 1855, in Upper Burma in 1867 and in Vietnam in 1874. In most of these cases the unequal treaties seemed to be at the time merely a phase in the onward expansion of Western influence. Yet the second phase of this expansion saw very different responses in different countries and, consequently, a different outcome. In the case of Japan, for example, the vigor of Japanese nationalism in the period of the Meiji Restoration led to the abolition of the unequal-treaty system by the end of the century. In Siam the British interest supported the continued independence and modernization of the Siamese nation without further foreign conquest. On the other hand, in Southeast Asia both Burma and the countries of Indochina became outright colonies. In the meantime, China in this second phase went into a status of even more obvious semicolonialism, in which by the end of the century the central-government revenues were in large part mortgaged to pay foreign debts and indemnities.

I think we may conclude that the process of imperialism in the latter part of the nineteenth century provided a very strong stimulus: one or two nations were able to respond with sufficient vigor to assert their nationalism, but the response of some countries for various reasons proved weaker, and the unequal treaties gave way to outright colonialism. One may suggest that imperialism in its early phase was primarily a stimulus and that only in its later phases, when not checked, did it become more definitely exploitative or depressive.

In this framework, the Chinese problem was how to become a nation-state, and the problem for the historian of Chinese modernization is how to account for the tardiness of this process. I shall not attempt to do so here, even in a few well-chosen words, but I think we can see certain persistent features in the traditional Chinese order which made it difficult for the Chinese empire to become a nation-state quickly. These features appear still to characterize the Chinese regime today and still to inhibit its integration into the larger world community.

The persistent features of the traditional order in China may be listed under several broad categories. First, there is the unity of state and culture under the imperial monarchy. According to this tradition, the Chinese polity and Chinese culture were ideally coterminous, so that all persons of Chinese culture were part of the Chinese empire and the Chinese empire normally embraced them within one state. This of course underlies, in part, the current objection of both Chinese regimes to the concept of what they call "two Chinas."

Second, the traditional Chinese empire had, in fact, an extensive bureaucratic administration, able to apply the central principles of Confucian government to the entire range of local circumstances within the empire. This has given Chinese administrators a very long-continued experience in the government of an enormous population over a wide area. For example, the imperial post might be carried by camel in the northwest or by sampan in the southeast, and yet its functioning was governed by basic principles administered from Peking. In the same way, the land tax and other revenue collections might consist of timber or furs in outlying regions, millet and kaoliang in the north, and rice or other products in the south, and yet the whole revenue system was managed according to the central government's fiscal arrangement. The diversity both of topography and climate and of peoples and customs between the East China Sea and the Pamir Mountains or between the Amur River and Hainan Island was greater than in the Roman Empire or any other centrally controlled territorial regime in history. Yet the techniques of government from a central point had been worked out over so many hundreds of years, under so many different dynasties, that a great tradition had been built up to permit effective administration. This undoubtedly has been in the background of the remarkable success of the Chinese Communist Party in consolidating its government on the mainland.

A third feature of the traditional government was its capacity to recruit an elite of highly indoctrinated and talented persons to serve as officials. In the old days, this process led through the examination system, based on the Confucian classics, to the status of degree holder or gentry, and from these degree holders the great part of the officialdom was then appointed. The examination system was a complex and many-leveled one in which the candidate had not only to qualify for each of the three main levels but also to qualify merely to keep his current status. Although there were many ways of rising to the top, including the opportunity to pay for lower level degrees instead of taking examinations, the great majority of officials came through the examination route. The result was that the system had great flexibility and could give opportunity to persons of means, such as merchants, without destroying the essential indoctrination of the elite in the Confucian system. The capacity of the Confucian classics to indoctrinate the literate individual cannot be overestimated. The basic system of social relationships they supported was by no means egalitarian. On the contrary, it was strongly hierarchic, and the three principal bonds (*san-kang*) provided for the subordination of minister to prince, of son to father, and wife to husband, in a quite authoritarian manner.

This is the basis for a fourth characteristic of the traditional Chinese order—the fact that it had such a large component of ideology. By this I mean that the orthodoxy perpetuated through the classical studies of the elite was a very large element, comparatively, in the preservation of the system. In effect, the Confucian type of government put so much stress on proper learning and orthodoxy of thought that it was able over long periods to lessen its reliance on coercion or violence. Thus, for example, the Confucian system maintained a family structure which prepared the individual to accept state authority just as he had accepted that of the patriarch in his family.

One cannot look at this traditional order without being impressed with its balance and self-sufficiency as a political-social pattern; Chinese scholars of many generations were themselves impressed with the perfection of their system. Since China had always remained the center of the East Asian world, and, at least in its own view, the center of proper civilization, a self-righteous conviction of Chinese superiority was inevitable. This Sinocentrism was very marked in China's relations with surrounding countries and certainly may be seen in the background of some of China's recent difficulties on the international scene.

The modernization of China against this background of traditional order has usually been recorded as a series of disasters and collapses. This, indeed, is the feeling left in the minds of modern Chinese after a century and a half of Western expansion and invasion. They and their forebears have witnessed the collapse of the centralized monarchy with the growth of regionalism and eventually warlordism. They have seen the discrediting of Confucianism, the abolition in 1905 of the examination system and with it, therefore, the gentry class, and finally the end of the dynasty itself and the imperial monarchy that was its focus. All this has been a record of humiliation sufficient to dismay any patriot and to produce an ineradicable sense of grievance against modern history. It is this sense of grievance, no doubt, which underlies the current vogue of seeing imperialism as the source of modern China's difficulties.

If, however, we look at the past century of Chinese history, we can, I think, perceive the growth of a modern order moving through a series of phases, for each of which we can point to certain signposts. For example, on the plane of ideas, the traditional order had lacked the concept of a nation-state in an equal and sovereign position among other nation states. It had lacked the concept of progress, and accordingly of economic growth, as a normal expectation. It had lacked a doctrine of individualism comparable to that developed in Europe. Yet, if we look back over the phases of modernization as they gradually come into view in China, we can see beginnings that also have made their contribution to the growth of a modern Chinese order. This growth has been cumulative and, of course, is thus far little studied, but I think it can be noted through certain representative personalities.

In looking at these relatively neglected increments of modernization, we might begin with Li Hung-chang and his acceptance of Western technology, for instance in his founding of China's first steamship line, the China Merchants' Steam Navigation Company, or his building of the Imperial Railroads of North China in the 1880s.

Another individual whose representative quality has usually been neglected is Robert Hart who, in the Chinese Imperial Maritime Customs Service, actually began a modern civil service. Earlier fiscal procedures had been based locally on tax farming so that individual officials collected what they could and paid the government what they had to, beginning with certain established quotas to which "contributions" might be added. This was part of the old system of personal government, and Hart plainly represented a British influence in his building up of a different concept of salaried civil service.

The principal individual to smuggle "progress" into Confucianism was K'ang Yu-wei, who overcame the Ch'ing ban on the activity of scholars in politics when he led the agitation for reform after the Sino-Japanese War of 1894–1895. His reinterpretation of Confucianism, following the New Text school of Confucian scholarship, was in many ways a tour de force and yet, by working from the inside as an individual at the top of the literary world, K'ang was able to launch Chnese thinking in new directions. It is apparently a fact that before his day the injection into Chinese thought of major Western political ideas had been in large part prevented by the difficulty of incorporating outside ideas into the Chinese writing system. At any rate, K'ang Yu-wei and his colleagues in the reform movement brought the scholar actively into politics.

The growth of nationalism as a conscious doctrine, opposed to the earlier culturalism of the old order, is most easily associated with Liang Ch'i-ch'ao. His stress upon the people as the principal subject of Chinese history is in a very modern vein and undoubtedly represents part of the pervasive Japanese influence on the Chinese revolution which set in after 1895. Liang Ch'i-ch'ao, while not wishing to get rid of the monarchy, was a leader in the introduction of modern political thought. The Japanese influence on him remains to be studied.

One individual who missed the chance to be a leader in history was the unfortunate Kuang-hsü Emperor, who died on November 14, 1908, according to report, just the day before his aunt, the empress dowager, died. If she had not had him killed, as appears to have been the case, the Kuang-hsü Emperor might well have provided the focus for a movement leading to a constitutional monarchy.

This, in turn, could have saved China a great deal of turmoil and difficulty.

The individual who represents the modernization of the political structure after the abolition of the monarchy is Sun Yat-sen, who succeeded with Soviet help in the early 1920s in establishing a party dictatorship as the eventual substitute for monarchic or dynastic dictatorship. Sun had early contemplated the need for a period of "tutelage," for training the Chinese people in modern government. He had thought of leadership by an elite, which seemed obviously necessary in the Chinese situation. The Leninist style of party dictatorship fitted his needs extremely well when he took it over with the advice and assistance of Borodin and others. While the Kuomintang as a party dictatorship retained certain features of an earlier day, its successor has become more purely "modern" in this respect. Mao Tse-tung, for example, betrays no apparent trace of nepotism

Chiang Kai-shek may be taken to represent the stage of political development in which the party army provides the necessary basis of power. This again represented the Soviet influence of the early 1920s, when Chiang rose to prominence as the one individual who had a clear concept of the central strategic value of an indoctrinated party army.

Others could, of course, be brought into this catalog to represent still other features of the process of reorganization of the Chinese traditional order. We may well ask, for example, what has been the contribution of Chairman Mao. For one thing, he has reasserted China's superiority. No doubt part of his leadership has rested in his capacity to stand forth as an independent leader, able to use ideas from abroad, applying them to the "concrete realities" of China. Perhaps his most evident contribution has been in

25

the establishment of the idea of the supremacy of man over nature through the application of scientific technology. In this he at first followed the Soviet model even to the point of disaster, as when the Chinese Communist program for industrial development was given an inadequate base of agricultural development.

Perhaps more remarkable as a contribution to the new order is the mobilization of the Chinese people under Mao. His incorporation of the populace in the state as politically active individuals has been marked by new political techniques. The mass organizations under the Chinese Communists have brought people into large structures which cut across the lines of government and territorial administration so that, for example, all labor, all youth, or all women can be motivated through their functional life in addition to being reached through territorial government. The combination of the military, the civil administration, and the Communist Party makes a tripod comparable to the tripod of the military, the civil bureaucracy, and the censorate under the dynastic regimes. But the mass organizations now form a fourth leg and create an even more extensive structure above the individual. By using the mass organizations, it is possible to mount campaigns or drives which indoctrinate and motivate each person, both in his thinking and in his conduct, for state purposes.

There are, of course, many points of conflict between the new order that has been growing up and the traditional Chinese order. For example, nineteenth-century Marxism-Leninism is a very different view of the world from the rather Legalist-tinged imperial Confucianism of the Ch'ing period. One can see today the conflict between Maoist doctrines of constant struggle and the old imperial doctrine of pervasive harmony. Where the traditional empire tried to inculcate the idea that peace must reign on all sides under the emperor's benevolence, now the regime at Peking seems to require "American imperialism" as a necessary enemy to struggle against.

One may also remark on Mao's revolutionary extremism. His belief in the capacity of the right doctrine to assist individuals to achieve liberation has led to an ongoing revolutionary effort that sometimes overleaps itself. Mao believes it possible to liberate the energies latent in the populace by getting rid of the stultifying influence of carlier "feudalism" or "imperialism" and thus to achieve miracles. In 1955, for example, he took the decision to press forward even faster with agricultural collectivization, and he similarly led the way in pushing the Great Leap Forward of 1958 and the simultaneous founding of communes. Both of these later developments fell short, and it has taken some time for the Chinese economy to revive.

Thus Mao's extremism has failed to consolidate the revolution and administer the new state on a basis of steady development. This would seem to indicate that dependence on the morale, first, of party members and cadres and, second, of the Chinese people as a whole is an unreliable feature of the new order. It is, in fact, a traditional feature in modern form. It consists in depending on the strong ideological component of the state system, instead of depending on a system of law as in the West. Mao's government is effective through moral suasion and manipulation. The elite works upon the people in general. But the regime lacks a tradition of the supremacy of law, or its codification and interpretation, to provide a steadying influence.

The pressure of population is another of Communist China's difficulties, and this material fact undoubtedly will create strains in the system. Millions of youth every year must be given employment, and as education progresses the expectations of youth may be increasingly frustrated.

The size of the population base is unprecedented in history, and its pressure upon the rather limited resources of the Chinese area creates a potentially explosive situation.

One can conclude that Communist China must develop its foreign trade or suffer stultification. In general, it will need to participate more actively in the new supranational world and this, of course, means contact. The American role in this cannot be decisive. The decision must come from Peking.

3 THE PEOPLE'S

MIDDLE KINGDOM

"Communist China"—how far Communist? How far Chinese? And what is the difference anyway? How are we to evaluate the impact that decades of war and violence and revolutionary zeal have had upon the China of today? Do Peking's leaders use the terminology of Marxism-Leninism-Maoism but express sentiments inherited from the Middle Kingdom? Are they unconsciously in the grip of their past, even when most explicitly condemning it? Certainly there is a resonance between China today and earlier periods. But how great is the actual continuity?

American expectations of Chinese behavior have groped along two lines—the approach by way of Moscow, the Soviet example, and the approach by way of history, Chinese tradition. The two overlap considerably, but both are faulted by discontinuity. China today is not just another Russia. It is very different indeed. Nor is the People's Republic just another imperial dynasty. Times have changed.

History can only help to synthesize these two approaches and suggest the degree of overlap. Chinese traditions, the

From *Foreign Affairs*, July 1966.

Soviet example, and the accidential conjunctions of events can all be given meaning in a chronological perspective. But history is invoked by all parties—by our Marxist adversaries, so addicted to their "world history," and by our own policy makers, particularly when we have to be aggressive. Even the stoutest pragmatists can hardly leave it alone. Yet history is an art, not a science, a game any number can play except historians, who feel too ignorant to play with self-confidence.

The first difficulty for all China pundits is the very high level of generality at which the game is played. Surely "Chinese history" offers "lessons" as diverse as the experience of a quarter of mankind during three thousand years. But we are all entangled in the old Chinese custom of viewing the Chinese realm, *t'ien-hsia* or "all under Heaven," as a unit of discourse. We still characterize dynastic periods—Han, T'ang, Sung, Ming, Ch'ing—as homogeneous slices of experience even when each lasted two or three hundred years. It is like a tenth-grade course on "Europe since the Fall of Rome." At such a level of generality, platitude is unavoidable. Statesmen who need an analytic scalpel are handed a sledgehammer.

Our second problem is the subjective factor. Appraising the impact of Communism on China is like studying the life of a man who got religion. He lives in the same house, with many of the same habits, and looks much the same. His conversion is greater subjectively, as judged by what he says, than objectively, as visible in his conduct. Yet his life has presumably taken a sharp turn and will never be the same again.

The degree of change in recent decades in China cannot be measured quantitatively but only by drawing a qualitative picture of a traditional model. This may then be compared with a similarly abstract contemporary model.

Changes of content will by definition be greater than changes of pattern.

China as seen in the middle of the nineteenth century was most remarkable for its great cultural self-consciousness, a sense of its own history. This ethos was held and perpetuated by the ruling class, best described as literati. The ruling stratum included nearly all people of substance and status, pre-eminently the holders of degrees gained through the official examinations or, in about one third of the cases, through purchase. From these degree holders were selected the actual officials, who totaled some twenty to forty thousand, depending on how one counts—in any case a remarkably small number considering that they governed a country of three or four hundred million people. The literate ruling class included on its lower level a large penumbra of landlords and merchants, since men of wealth could buy degree status by their contributions to government. At its top level, it included the aristocracy created by the dynasty and the dynasty itself with the emperor at its apex.

Mobility into and out of this ruling stratum gave it strength and durability. The government's philosophy was to preserve itself by recruiting the able. The ruler's chief task was to find men of talent. Unusual talent could rise.

This old Chinese government was hard for Westerners to understand because it really operated at two levels, one official and the other informal. On the official level the emperor and his bureaucracy kept a monopoly of all the symbols of authority, and sat on top of all large-scale activities. The government not only dominated education through the examination system; it had long since broken up the Buddhist church and kept Taoism and Buddhism decentralized in isolated units across the countryside. The secular faith of Confucianism was expounded under official auspices in the Confucian temples. The officials kept all merchant enterprises under their control by the simple device of squeezing the merchants, and absorbing them into the official class when they got big enough. All large-scale public works were, of course, governmental. The emperor patronized the arts and had the greatest collections of both art and literature. He censored literature with a heavy hand to suppress anti-Manchu works. The emperor as a high priest conducted sacrifices to the forces of nature at the temples of heaven and of agriculture at Peking. He was also the high exemplar of the religion of filial piety so stressed in the Confucian classics. His prerogatives covered everything and made him potentially the strongest monarch who had ever lived.

Yet this formal government by its small size was necessarily very superficial. It ruled without a rival, but it did not penetrate the villages. They were the scene of an informal or unofficial kind of government, headed by the gentry degree holders in each locality. The local elite cooperated with the few local magistrates to maintain the social order. They were examination-oriented, always eager to encourage talent that might rise to power. Meantime, they stood for stability and felt an obligation to keep city walls, moats, bridges, roads, and temples in repair, to encourage private schooling within the family clan, and even in time of need to organize public relief and raise militia to maintain order.

This local-gentry tradition has only begun to be studied. It included a good deal of local initiative and clan spirit, if not indeed public spirit. Gentry scholars compiled thousands of local histories or gazetteers and family genealogies. They had a secular faith in the Confucian social order. They denounced all improper conduct, heterodoxy, and the subversiveness of missionaries with their doctrines of egalitarianism. Gentry and officialdom were at one in supporting a society of status. They did not believe in individualism or equality as abstract principles, but stressed the duties of all good men functioning in their proper niches in the social hierarchy.

The main object of government at both the official and unofficial levels was to perpetuate itself and the social order by living off the peasants and, at the same time, maintaining their welfare. The peasantry being illiterate were politically passive, since political action in this bureaucratic society was through the written word if at all. The peasant village happily never saw an official and dealt with his tax-gatherers only periodically. Though illiterate, the villagers of course had a rich culture of folklore and custom, religious faith and superstition, and complex interpersonal relations within and between families. Our picture of this folk society is still seen largely through Confucian glasses. It was, of course, pre-modern and cut off from the outside world. The peasant economy used a highly developed man-power technology that had accumulated over millennia. In good crop years life went on with much stability and many satisfactions; the Confucian ideals of social order had thoroughly permeated the society. Even bandits could follow the norms long since mirrored in some of the vernacular novels. Secret societies had their own ancient traditions. Both Buddhism and Taoism had a message for the old wives, and everyone knew that talent, assiduity, frugality, and loyalty to family and friends could help one get along.

This traditional society was mature within the limits of its pre-modern technology and so had a high degree of homeostasis or capacity to maintain a steady equilibrium. It was therefore ill-suited to modernization. The Jesuits pictured it to the European Enlightenment as an example of social harmony guided by ethics. But the law, for example, as Western merchants discovered at Canton, was administered purely as a tool of state and society, not to protect individual rights. It penalized a multitude of infractions of the social order, but obliged the magistrate to add in extralegal considerations in each case. The letter of the law was obscure or contradictory, and held in low esteem in comparison with ethical principles. Going to law was also bad news for all concerned because of official exactions. Litigation was thus a *pis aller,* and the law was no help to economic growth.

Much more could be said about our traditional model.. Sinologues East and West, ever since Ennin visited T'ang China from Japan in 838–947 and Marco Polo served there under the Mongols in 1275–1292, have never ceased trying to describe the curiously different Chinese way, a topic as enduring in Western culture as utopianism and the limits of state authority. One's main impression in retrospect today, I think, is of the strong Chinese feeling for "the social order," not "individualism," as the basis of welfare and the good life.

Down through the seventeenth and eighteenth centuries, China's evolution continued along established lines. The Ch'ing dynasty rounded out its frontiers across Inner Asia by subjugating the Western Mongols, Sinkiang, and Tibet. The Manchu rulers at Peking further perfected their control over domestic administration with all its checks and balances. China was at peace within, and the population apparently grew by leaps and bounds. Meanwhile, the Europeans moved into the successive phases of their modern revolution, both in science and technology and in national political development. The commercial and industrial revolutions began to overrun the earth. China, at the end of the line, was soon beleaguered.

By the late nineteenth century, the inadequacies of the traditional Chinese model were very plain to see. There was no ideal of progress, no sanction for economic gain and growth, no independence for the merchant or legal protection of his enterprise against official exactions. China was not able to transplant modern industry as Japan was doing, and consequently could not build adequate military power. Her great society fell behind. Westerners became entrenched in the centers of foreign trade, the treaty ports, and continued to dominate the processes of modernization.

Most obviously, this was a political problem. The Ch'ing dynasty failed to assert its central control over the economic and social processes that modernization encouraged. Partly it lacked the resources and skills, partly the idea, which the Japanese leaders had got from abroad. In the last analysis the Ch'ing leadership lacked the desire to remake China's traditional society on a foreign model. This was an innate disability, due to China's long history of superiority in her East Asian world. Sitting at the feet of the barbarians was more than Chinese pride could take.

At the same time, however, China's political weakness in the late nineteenth century was an accident of history, because of the declining vigor of the dynasty and the rise of rebellions borne on the back of population pressure. The Taipings and other rebels of the 1850s and '60s almost finished off the Peking regime. It made its peace with the foreigners in order to survive and to conquer the rebels. Thereafter it had to accept the foreigners as partners in modernization. But, unlike the Japanese, the Ch'ing leadership never really accepted the idea of mastering the foreign-invented processes of modernization and so controlling China's fate, as the Communists are now attempting to do. Instead, unable like Japan to modernize the state and abolish foreign privilege, China fell victim to foreign exploitation in the eventual age of imperialism at the turn of the century.

Traditional China collapsed over a long period with many bangs and whimpers. The emperor's supremacy over all men was tarnished by the post-Opium War treaties of the 1840s and denied by the second settlement of 1858–1860. Yet tribute missions continued to come to Peking until 1908. The transition was gradual. China did not send ministers abroad until the 1870s, and then only grudgingly. She entered the family of nations only part way. Thus her imperial claims to supremacy in East Asia were maintained side by side with the unequal treaties that put China in a semicolonial position vis-à-vis the West. This mixed order lasted fifty years.

The imperial institution, keystone of the old social order, finally came under attack from Chinese nationalism. Since the Manchus' incapacity to meet the modern challenge had led to China's humiliation, the revolutionaries of the 1900s, by a non sequitur, denounced the monarchy as the source of China's weakness. In 1911–1912 they threw out bath, bathtub, baby and all. Abolishing the monarchy had the effect of decapitating the society and created a serious vacuum of leadership.

Meanwhile the teachings of Confucius had suffered attrition. New learning from the West undermined the old faith. Missionaries gained few converts but their preachings of egalitarianism, individualism, science, and democracy were lent credence by the superior firepower of foreign gunboats. By the time the peripheral states that had normally been tributary to the Chinese court had become Western colonies, it was plain that the old order was doomed. As the gentry class disintegrated, after the examinations were abolished in 1905, new classes began to arise. Meanwhile the economy had been oriented more toward foreign trade through the new treaty ports; urbanization had grown with new factories and communications; and learning from abroad, especially from Japan, had become the accepted panacea. By the end of World War I, China had lost not only her secular faith of Confucianism, but also the formal government headed by the emperor with his broad prerogatives, and even the informal leadership of the local-gentry elite. The swollen numbers of the peasantry were living precariously. Talent had some new outlets but few established channels. Warlords in regional bases were wrecking the processes of government. Foreign influences were everywhere, and the great tradition was in the melting pot.

The humiliating weakness and confusion of the warlord era gave the Westerners of the last generation a stereotype of China as "a heap of loose sand" or "a mere geographical expression." It also impelled patriotic youth to support a revival of central power. A new nationalism swept China in the 1920s. The overriding consideration was how to achieve national self-respect. Western influences were providing a stimulus for individualism, for the emancipation of women to allow them to control their own marriages and become educated, for the study of science and adoption of technology to achieve "progress." There was a recognition of Western superiority in many ways. All sorts of ideas flooded in and were taken up. But the deep-down concern was for the national glory. One could not be Chinese without having a dedicated conviction of the innate worth and superiority of Chinese culture. A strong state to provide a home for it was the first essential.

37

This new nationalism converged with or overlapped the traditional urge to reunify the state after the collapse of a dynasty. The forty years from the end of the Ch'ing in 1912 to the Communist takeover of 1949 is about the standard length of a dynastic interregnum in earlier instances. There had been comparable periods of disorder at the end of the T'ang, the Sung, and the (Mongol) Yuan dynasties. The consolidation of Ch'ing power took forty years from the seizure of Peking in 1644 to the last suppression of rebels in 1683. In every such period, there eventually arose a universal demand for a return to peace and order under central authority. By the end of World War II in China, this had become a widespread longing.

The rebuilding of central power was, of course, not merely a Communist achievement but began with the Kuomintang. Sun Yat-sen based his revolution on the foreign edge of China, using the funds of overseas Chinese merchants in Malaya and Hawaii, recruiting the patriotism and eloquence of students abroad in Japan and Europe, mounting his ten putsches from around the edge of China with arms smuggled in to secret societies allied with him. Yet he found that the democratic West could give him all the equipment and methods of modernization except the essential one of organizing power in post-dynastic China. He found constitutions of little use, warlord armies unreliable no matter how good their weapons, and parliamentary parties as friable as the politicians who joined them, without constituencies and without loyalty to any common authority. By 1919 Sun was convinced that his revolution, if it was to make any comeback at all, must be led by a reorganized party. He found a model for this in Leninism, and Soviet delegates helped him organize the Kuomintang in the early 1920s at the same time that they helped the Chinese Communist Party come into being in 1921.

The competition between the Kuomintang and the Chinese Communists in the 1920s, which has almost monopolized the attention of historians, was never as close a race as some have liked to think. There was no real competition at first between Sun Yat-sen's many thousands of middle-aged revolutionaries and the few dozens or hundreds of young Communist students. By 1927 the Nationalist reunification had succeeded up to a point, and the social revolution of the Communists was deferred. Apparently China was ready for the former but not for the latter. The new student class and the merchants in the cities were most aware of the foreign "imperialist" presence and most moved by the new nationalism, whereas the crisis in peasant life and the breakup of the old family system in the villages were not yet in the forefront of concern.

The first move in rebuilding a central government was the establishment of a party dictatorship and a party army to support it. This was achieved under the national government at Canton in the early 1920s, in Sun Yat-sen's last years. Many of the Cantonese and other leaders in his group accepted Lenin's theory of imperialism and were united by antiforeignism but abjured the class struggle within the nation. Out of Canton, as head of the Northern Expedition to unify China, came Chiang Kai-shek. It is now evident that his rise was due not merely to a talent for political-military manipulation, but also to his devotion to the primary cause of the day, national reunification. For this he saw the indoctrinated party army as the essential tool, acting on behalf of the Kuomintang dictatorship. China's nominal reunification under the Nanking government in 1928 thus marked the first great institutional step of substituting party dictatorship for dynastic rule.

This transition, with all its modern potentialities, now permitted the state for the first time to penetrate the villages. Twentieth-century China had inherited a polity that was highly authoritarian but superficial. Modern totalitarianism has been achieved by expanding the old authoritarianism down into the body social—mobilizing, activating, and manipulating a populace that was formerly inert in politics and parochial in its interests. Among so vast a public, this has been a slow process. In addition to the practical concerns of livelihood that induce modernization, it has been motivated by national pride. One result of mass participation has been a dilution of quality and lowering of standards in the first instance. If we compare the building of China's new order with the old structure sketched above, we will be struck by the simultaneous revival of old patterns and creation of new content to fit into them.

The transition from dynastic to party rule, at least in theory, had taken only sixteen years, from 1912 to 1928. It shows considerable continuity in the midst of discontinuity. Dynasties and parties have in common, first, a definable and ongoing group of power holders, whether it is a harem-produced swarm of princes or a central committee thrown up by the intraparty political struggle. Second, this ongoing group selects, not without much interplay of pressures, the top executive and assists him in running the government. The top man, Chinese-style, has to be both a sage and a hero, enunciating the ideology, making the final decisions and ruling in person, not just reigning. He must be a model of propriety and the patron of art and letters, even a poet, as well as the arbiter of disputes and maintainer of morale. His ideological pronouncements are important because his rule is still very personal, by moral teaching more than by legal process. Personal loyalty still plays a role.

Finally, the structure of government is still similar. The military is quite separate from the civil administration but both are headed by the One Man. Meanwhile there is a third, separate, echelon of supervisory personnel. In the old days it included palace eunuchs as well as dynastic family members and the whole establishment of the Censorate, both at the capital and in the provinces. Both Chiang and Mao have sat on the ancient tripod of civil bureaucracy, army, and supervisory agencies, which now include secret police and informers as well as the party apparatus.

Discontinuity, of course, is most evident in the substitution of Marxism-Leninism-Maoism for imperial Confucianism, of a dialectic doctrine of struggle instead of harmony. Yet we should not overlook the pattern of orthodoxy so evident in both cases: the faith in a true teaching revealed in classical works, the role of the One Man or Leader as their expositor, the recruitment of talent as tested by the orthodox teaching, and the constant indoctrination of the entire government apparatus as a means of giving it unity and keeping it under control. Talent is still recruited and examined; a bureaucratic career still requires qualities of loyalty, obedience, and finesse in personal relations; and heterodoxy is still condemned and attacked.

One principal change comes from the expansion of politics. Every village now participates in the political life that was formerly reserved for the ruling class. Peasant passivity has given way to activism by all citizens. Where a dynasty used to claim it ruled the Middle Kingdom with the Mandate of Heaven, now the "people" are said to make their own destiny through their chosen (?) instrument, the Chinese Communist Party. One of Mao's departures from Marxism-Leninism is to assert that the party leads China's

41

regeneration not only on behalf of the proletariat but also on behalf of a coalition of major classes—in effect, the whole people.

Without attempting further to describe it, one can only conclude from the outside that the content of the new orthodoxy is a far cry indeed from the comparatively static doctrines of Confucian self-discipline within an immutable social order inherited from the golden age of antique sages. Having supplanted the forces of nature or "Heaven," the "people" are now viewed as the vital makers of history, brimming with creative capacities. The Maoist leadership with its insight can liberate these long latent "productive forces." The new China is science-minded, people-minded, dynamic and convinced of its own creativity.

Yet this new order still subordinates the individual. Chinese youth escaped the family only to come under the small group, the production team, the party, and the nation. From the first Mao has warred against individualism as the germ of bourgeois thinking. Civil liberties piously listed in state documents are reserved for the "people," not for those viewed by authority as "enemies of the people." An accused has few judicial rights—how can his petty interest outweigh that of all the rest of the Chinese people? Law still lacks any sanctity or even a codified and publicized content and reliable procedure. People's courts and procurators steer by political considerations as well as by Mao's normative pronouncements and administrative regulations. The authoritarianism of the traditional state left little sanction for individualism, and the Communists do not propose to supply any now.

Just here, however, history perhaps has a message for us. The old China, in daily life below the official level, was humane in many senses of the term. The ideal "superior man" (*chün-tzu*), whose learned and proper conduct entitled him to public prestige and leadership, was not merely a servant of state authority. When not in office he pursued self-cultivation (*hsiu-shen*), calligraphy, and poetry, even philosophic meditation. The old Chinese compulsion to train oneself in literary and other accomplishments was not purely repressive self-discipline but created one's capacity for friendship and personal enjoyment. Confucian humanism had a long tradition, albeit within a collectivist social order, and peasants who today join in politics, as only the "superior man" used to do, may some time also aspire on a mass scale to the self-cultivation that was once the hallmark of the gentry elite. The historical adage that revolutions after their excesses swing back toward past norms has received some support from Soviet revisionism, and Peking's fulminations against it make it seem a bit more probable for China in due time.

Continuity is thus a matter of degree. So much remains of the old landscape and its many problems: the Yellow River still flows five hundred miles across the North China Plain, silting its bed above the level of the fields. There are still the precarious rainfall in the northwest and the danger of drought and famine, the weaknesses of a capital-poor and labor-intensive farm economy, the need to keep up morale and "nourish honesty" (*yang-lien*) as of old among so far-flung a bureaucracy. Chairman Mao's vision of betterment must still be achieved inside a society that has a deeply ingrained inheritance, more profoundly imbedded than either we or even Chairman Mao, from our opposite sides, may realize. It is represented, for instance, in the Chinese ideographic writing system, which it seems cannot be changed into a more flexible alphabetic or other purely phonetic system.

Even the most iconoclastic new leaders, facing these problems, will be tempted to revive traditional ways of

43

meeting them, like the well-worn device of mutual responsibility that sets neighbor spying on neighbor within a street committee. Whatever the leaders may hope, the people by their responses, less creative than the leadership, may revive old ways under new names. Certain continuities like pride of culture may well up in a resurgent nationalism that no man can control. It is in this context that we must view Peking's recent series of remarkable disasters in foreign relations.

It is a truism that the Long March generation now in power have been spiritually in combat all their lives and are psychologically struggle-prone. By 1949 their heavenstorming militancy had picked the United States, the biggest thing in sight, as their implacable foe. By 1960 they had added the Soviet Union. This imprudent and irrational course has been justified by Mao and explained by outside observers partly on ideological grounds. Mao's doctrinaire extremism has not only challenged the Chinese people to superhuman efforts; it also keeps the Leninist faith intact.

But the vehemence of Peking's denunciations of the two outside worlds that now encircle the embattled People's Middle Kingdom (*Jen-min Chung-kuo*) seems more than "ideological" in the usual sense of the term. Such impassioned scorn, such assertive righteousness, also echo the dynastic founders of ages past.

Founding a dynasty required a man larger than life, and several great dynasties were put together by individuals with some touch of paranoia. The unifiers of the Ch'in in 221 B.C. and the Sui in 589 A.D. pulled the empire together in fevered bursts of energy. The founder of the Ming who threw out the Mongols in 1368 also had illusions of grandeur, cut off heads, liked to have errant ministers ceremoniously beaten in court, built vast walls and palaces, and got all East Asia to send him tribute missions. This fanaticism was in the minority tradition of emperors who conquer by the sword and organize manpower to build great public works—a Great Wall, a Grand Canal—rather than in the majority tradition of those who consolidate and rule through the bureaucracy. Dynastic founders were often great blueprint artists who reorganized Chinese society according to dogmatic plans and visionary doctrines. They were usually followed by consolidators who tidied up the regime and eventually let the people relax.

Mao's hostile extremism today toward an outside world that he only vaguely discerns must be seen as a function or offshoot of his extremism within his own country. Remaking China, remolding all of its people, building a modern state power, are all-absorbing tasks. No one else in world history has ever tackled such a big job, for no other country has ever been so big and so materially backward. Mao's considerable achievement—everyone fed, everyone marching—is a triumph not of cool calculation but of vision and will, as he is not the last to proclaim. In this violent process of constant and induced "struggle," ideology is a factor in its own right but also a tool of that more protean collective impulse we inadequately call "national ism." We could equally well call it Sinocentrism in modern dress.

Xenophobic contempt for foreign cultures became a standard part of China's long-conditioned response to the power of the Inner Asian barbarians. Until 1860, barely a century ago, China's leaders had suffered many times under foreign rule but had never met an equal, much less a superior, foreign culture. The old political myth of China's superiority was based on solid cultural realities even when inspired also by a need to rationalize military weakness. Today, to expect Chinese patriots to acknowledge a double weakness, both cultural and material, in both basic principles and practical devices, the *t'i* and the *yung* discussed by early reformers, is asking too much. They will sooner claim they have what China needs and condemn the outside world as evil, fit only for salvation through Maoist-type subversion.

In short, Peking's intractable mood comes out of China's history, not just from Lenin's book.

PART II

THE TAIWAN PROBLEM

4 COMMUNIST CHINA

AND TAIWAN IN U.S.

FOREIGN POLICY

The rise of a new leadership in Washington in 1960 gave
us a creative opportunity to look at the rise of Communist
China in a new and broader perspective. First, in the perspective of American party politics, Kennedy's election
presumably marked the burial of that unreal and divisive
issue, "Who lost China?" In the game of "Who lost what?"
too many other, more recent, equally unreal "losses" took
precedence—for example, "Who lost Cuba?" or "Who lost
the missile race?" Consequently China policy never really
figured in the 1960 election, except for the minor issue as
to whether we should try to lose Quemoy ahead of time, as
Kennedy suggested, or lose it only after defending it, as
Richard Nixon would have had us do. That an essentially
tactical problem like Quemoy was the principal aspect of
China policy brought up for debate underlined the basic
fact that both parties had been so lacking in any real China

The Brien McMahon Lecture, University of Connecticut, November 21,
1960; reprinted by permission of the University.

policy in recent years that we could all start afresh in 1961 from a position of general bankruptcy.

Second, in the perspective of history, our so-called traditional China policy, that of the Open Door for trade and the integrity of China as a nation, is now equally bankrupt. As an attitude of good will it did us credit; as a diplomatic policy enshrined in the Washington Conference Nine-Power Treaty of 1922, it became a liability, because thereafter it was not backed up by any adequate naval and strategic policy. After 1922 we were committed to support China's "territorial and administrative integrity"; yet when Japan attacked China in 1931 we lacked both the power and the purpose to do so by force. The result was the humiliating and unsettling decade of drift from 1931 to 1941, when we gave material support to Japanese militarism by continuing to trade with Japan, and gave moral support to Nationalist China by continuing to denounce Japanese militarism. During the 1930s our combination of the Open Door policy on paper with an ignoble isolationism in fact prepared the way for cataclysmic results in the 1940s—the destruction of the better, nonmilitarist part of Nationalist China by Japan, the eventual destruction of Japanese militarism by us, and the defeat of Nationalist China's residual postwar militarism by the rise of the Chinese Communists.

Today the Open Door is shut from both sides. It is no longer our aim to support the national integrity of mainland China. Our support of the integrity of Free China on Taiwan may, by some, be considered a continuation of our traditional Open Door policy. But the existence of an independent Chinese government on Taiwan must actually be recognized, by all but antiquarians, as a new fact of international life. It requires a new approach which is neither tailored to the opportunist needs of American party politics nor stuck sentimentally in a dead tradition.

If we are to move forward in the 1960s we must have still another perspective, and that is on ourselves and our emotional involvement with the fate of China. This also is at a dead end, for the Chinese people under Chinese Communism are even farther removed from our influence than the Russian people under Soviet Communism. This has been so increasingly for ten years, but it takes us a long time to lose the Sinophile feeling that the American people are the special patrons and protectors of the Chinese people.

This special emotional involvement of ourselves with China (call it Sinophilism?) dies slowly because it has had a long history. Back of it lies a century of missionary interest and activity which had several peculiar features. First, missionary concern about China remained strongest in the Middle West, curiously enough in the very region that in the 1930s remained most strongly isolationist toward Europe. Second, American missionaries in China pursued their good works under the protection of extraterritoriality and the other special privileges of the unequal-treaty system. This inevitably made them somewhat too much mixed up with the old order. Third, their good works gave the initial stimuli to many aspects of China's modernization, and so, paradoxically, they were early patrons of revolutionary change in China, but destined in the end to become its victims. Fourth, this missionary concern for China-as-it-used-to-be eventually had political repercussions in the United States. During the course of one hundred years our missionaries gradually got China included within the vague confines of the American liberal dream of a better future, on the hopeful assumption that what was good for America would be good for China. The American public began to feel that we played an essential and benevolent role in Chinese life, as indeed we sometimes did or were made by Chinese friends to feel that we did. Americans began to identify themselves with China's fortunes more fully than with most foreign situations.

In the 1930s many hoped they saw in the Nationalist Government a leadership striving not only for national power but also for individual freedom and betterment. In the late 1930s and early 1940s some Americans, disillusioned with Nanking, hoped they could see some promise of liberalism among the Chinese Communists at Yenan. Both of these hopes, the more positive one about the Nationalists and the less real one about the Communists, were thoroughly frustrated by history in 1949. In retrospect, given all the circumstances of the time, they seem to have been projections onto China of an American dream which could not be realized in the face of China's ancient tradition and modern difficulties.

As a result of all this, American feelings about China were rudely shocked by the rise of the Chinese Communists. The chief foreign recipients of our religious good will and good works, the Chinese people, seemed in 1949 to have rejected us. China not only did not go Christian— it actually went Communist. I suggest that this contributed to the demoralization of the McCarthy era. American liberalism in the early 1950s had no adequate explanation for this deeply frustrating emotional disaster in China, and no solution to advocate. It was bankrupt of ideas about how to meet the problem of communism in China and therefore had no answer with which to check the exploitation by McCarthy and McCarran of the "loss" of China. A feeling of outraged and embattled frustration lives on in the person of such Republican orators as the former China missionary, ex-Congressman Walter Judd.

However, no amount of nostalgic feeling can give us an adequate China policy for the nuclear age of the 1960s. Entirely new principles are needed for this unprecedented epoch. For the dangerous future we have one overriding national interest, to avoid surrender while at the same time avoiding nuclear disaster, or at least mitigating the destruction which use of nuclear weapons will cause. Our sometimes shadowy concept of national interest is thus starkly simplified. We seek to survive without surrendering or being too badly damaged, and this interest is roughly the same as that of every other people.

This interest dictates dual aims, to build up the institutions and practices of a world order and at the same time to maintain the boundaries and the political health of the non-Communist part of the world; in practical terms, to achieve arms control and to maintain a frontier within which free institutions may be nurtured. These general aims have been eloquently stated by many others. How do they apply to our China policy?

To begin with, our regional policy for East Asia no longer differs from our policy elsewhere (as the Open Door used to differ from our nonentanglement with Europe), but is part of a global policy. Let me continue by stating certain assumptions. In East Asia we must first of all defend a boundary to keep Japan from Communist absorption because a Communist Japan with its industrial skills, even more than a Communist India, would tip the world power balance and have us soon fighting for survival. Defense of South Korea and of Taiwan are, incidentally, related to the problem of defending Japan.

Second, in East Asia we must aim to build up institutions of international order and, as part of this, get Peking sooner or later into a system of arms control. As a preliminary step, of course, such a system has to be inaugurated with Moscow. Unless it is, neither we nor the Russians have much hope of a happy old age.

My next assumption is that to achieve this overriding purpose of arms control, Peking's entry in some fashion into the United Nations will probably be useful. It will be no panacea. But as time goes on, Peking's continued exclusion from the United Nations will become more difficult for us to maintain. The problem is not made easier by the probability, as we must assume, that Peking would prefer to enter the United Nations over our opposition and through our defeat. "American imperialism" has seemed this far to be a necessary, semipermanent enemy in Peking's ideology and operations. Nevertheless we face alternatives of world order or world chaos, and the world must eventually include mainland China.

Supposing that we can make some progress with the Soviets toward arms control, as a step toward world order, then the essential preliminary to getting Peking into the United Nations on constructive terms would be fairly plain —namely, we would have to get both Peking and Taipei willing to accept international status for Taiwan as an independent republic. For this purpose Peking would have to acknowledge Taiwan's independence, at least tacitly. This kind of outcome is now loudly denounced in both Peking and Taipei; yet it seems to be the only way to end the Chinese civil war. It amounts to formal recognition of the status quo which has obtained ever since 1949. It seeks stability in East Asia based on a rough balance of power: we would support islands and peninsulas in the Western Pacific, and whatever more we could, against the growing power of mainland China.

These assumptions may be recapitulated as follows, each one conditional on the one before: (1) sooner or later, human survival will require an effective arms-control agreement with Soviet Russia, which (2) will require Peking's adherence, which (3) will require Peking's admission to the international order of the United Nations, which (4) will require Taiwan's being acknowledged an independent state, which (5) will be just exactly contrary to what

54

both Peking and Taipei have been saying, with their usual remarkable prescience, for many years past. This sequence of five points offers a solution to our China problem. The only thing lacking is its acceptance by any Chinese on either side.

Perhaps this lack of any Chinese concurrence in what seems to many Westerners to be a dandy scheme marks the cultural gap between Western and Chinese political ideas and values. Perhaps, on the other hand, these are positions for bargaining, which Chinese of both camps have preempted. Since in the ancient tradition of bargaining, in China as elsewhere, an asking price is not a final bid, let us keep this sequence of five possibilities in mind and examine several questions bearing on them—first of all, how does Taiwan figure in our over-all policy?

My own belief is that Taiwan is the key to our China policy in general. Communist China cannot be given any kind of status in the international world without Taiwan's being given a new status too. The two problems are interlocked.

Taiwan still probably has some importance in military strategy. But its chief importance is in our diplomatic strategy, in the diplomacy of power politics. We should not delude ourselves with the customary American hope that we can get a settlement with Communist China which is anything more than an equilibrium, a confrontation of forces in continuing stalemate, a constant low-level tension, which is the modern substitute for peace. Nevertheless, low tension may be preferable to high tension.

Today Taiwan is the main issue between Peking and us. Peking could find others, but Taiwan is an ideal issue: (1) India and other non-Communist Asians still regard Taiwan nominally as part of China, a domestic Chinese issue. (2) So does Chiang Kai-shek, who seeks, not independence from China, but China. (3) Peking can rouse mainland chauvinism among the Chinese people against the Taiwan threat and yet be excused for inability to cross a hundred miles of water without a navy.

On Taiwan, American and Nationalist aims are divergent, as they were during World War II. Then, we aimed to defeat Japan, while Chiang aimed also to stay in power and later defeat the Communists. Now, our aim (largely unexpressed) is to maintain a Free China in being, while Chiang's (as expressed) is to wait for a chance at reconquest. What are our reasons for supporting Taiwan?

Our immediate cold-war aim is defensive, to avoid losing another area to Communism, and also military, for intelligence work and maintenance of an armed base on the flank of any Chinese Communist expansion southward. (On these points Chiang agrees with us.) These aims are immediate, unavoidable, and in the foreground but should not obscure larger, more constructive long-term aims which have been kept generally in the background.

As a simple moral issue, we cannot abandon thirteen million Taiwan Chinese to the lower living standard, reprisals, and remolding process which they would inevitably suffer under Chinese Communism.

More constructively, for the long term we must always remember that the Chinese people form a cultural entity, distinctive and apart, of very large size, almost a quarter of mankind. We want *contact* with some part of this Chinese world that is friendly to us, that can be our window on Chinese life, a place to train our China specialists, a source of Chinese talent for us to train, a center for study of the mainland through Chinese eyes, so that in general we will not be completely out of touch with the Chinese quarter of mankind and their distinctive culture and consequently be less able to deal with them. This is a residue left over from our traditional China policy.

In our long-term political strategy, we want to help a non-Communist Chinese area grow and develop, not necessarily as a military threat, but as a pilot-model competitor, a place where non-Communist Chinese economic growth, non-Communist Chinese political development, and non-Communist learning (an image of China) can set an example. To this we want to give our support. In Taiwan today the Joint Commission on Rural Reconstruction sets just such an example in agricultural development.

As Soviet-American competition becomes more ideological (beyond the material military-economic plane on which both sides offer rather similar wares), we must approach all Asia with a picture of the modern world and its history more meaningful than Marxism-Leninism. The non-Communist explanation of the social process—of imperialism, colonialism, nationalism, economic growth, social order—must make more sense to Asians than the Communist explanation. However, Americans alone cannot grasp and express the meaning of modernization in Asia, but only by working with Asian scholars, journalists, artists, writers, and leaders. For East Asia the dominant intellectual problem is to appraise Communist China—is it a tragedy of history, or East Asia's future? Taiwan, with its research scholars and essential modern history archives, is already becoming a base for this intellectual development.

With a constructive Sino-American program, Taiwan can give the non-Communist world all these advantages of contact and competition, as an unsinkable military-defense, political, and cultural base, at comparatively low cost. The hundred miles of water in the Formosa Straits form the most defensible barrier on the frontier of any major power, close enough for some contact, too far for invasion.

In short, for all these reasons we are indissolubly involved in the defense and support of Taiwan for the foreseeable future. Our problems are (1) how to give Taiwan a more realistic and secure international status and (2) how to get Chiang Kai-shek and the Kuomintang to modify their aims enough to share our aims more fully. These problems must be faced now, at the same time that we try to deal with the Communist China problem.

This brings me to a much-neglected question of practical tactics and day-to-day procedures in the execution of our China policy. It is time to ask whether American representatives, even the best, are capable of dealing, man for man, with their Chinese counterparts without losing at least their shirts and probably more. It does not require much reflection, on the part of American negotiators who have had the experience, to realize after the fact, when it is too late, how consistently they have been outmaneuvered by Chinese diplomats and political leaders in the past. This is because Americans are only the most recent in a long succession of foreigners who have been manipulated by ancient Chinese methods for dealing with foreigners.

Chiang Kai-shek and Mao Tse-tung are both ethnocentric patriots (Mao perhaps to a lesser extent), more traditional in their feelings than we usually realize—focused, first of all, on Chinese politics, especially their own party politics, and the art of keeping personal power by manipulating followers and enemies alike. Now Chinese politics are more subtle and sophisticated, if less vocal, more personal and less ideological, than Western politics, which explains why so many American envoys have been frustrated, flattered, confused, or enthusiastic in the course of their negotiations, but seldom victorious over Chinese interests. General Marshall, for example, defeated Germany and Japan but not Chiang Kai-shek. This was because Chiang stayed on his home ground, in his own terrain of Chinese politics, where he was sovereign and General Marshall an outsider. Any ambassador in Taipei is on the same spot, an outsider participating in a Chinese scene he cannot fully penetrate or intellectually control. A Soviet ambassador in Peking is in a similar position.

In Taipei, for example, people are still arguing today about how it happened that the American Embassy there was so thoroughly sacked and looted of secrets by an organized, uncontrolled student mob a few years ago—was it an accident or a plot, and if so by whom? Actually it was only an incident in the process of keeping the American Embassy under control. Similarly, Peking's quarrel with Khrushchev immediately increased Communist China's nuisance value within the Communist world.

Chinese operating principles for the manipulation of "barbarians" are not improvised like our policies of recent times, but are inherited from a great tradition that comes down from centuries even before the Mongols and Manchus conquered and ruled all China. From ancient times the sedentary Chinese farmers and bureaucrats have always had to deal from weakness with powerful, mobile, non-Chinese fighters and conquerors. Today, Chiang deals with us from weakness, while Mao deals with the Russians, also from weakness. Both are doing well.

1. The cardinal Chinese principle in dealing with a non-Chinese is to use friendship as a halter. Admit the outsider to a guest membership in Chinese society. Compliment him on his knowledge of aspects of Chinese culture or of the Chinese language. Entertain him with informality and frankness. Establish the personal bonds of friendship, which in the old China were stronger than in Western urban life today. Become really intimate friends and understand his unspoken assumptions and personal motivations.

2. Ask the foreigner's advice so as both to ascertain his

aims and values and to enlist his sympathy and support. (Both these principles help to account for our Sinophilism.)

3. Disclose to him those Chinese vital interests which are allegedly more important than life itself, so as to pre-empt a position ahead of time and warn him it is not negotiable.

4. Build up the peculiar uniqueness of Chinese values and conduct (as I am doing here) so as to suggest the dangers of stormy unpredictability, preternatural stubborness, or other traits of the powerholder, which present the foreigner with insuperable difficulties.

5. Find out the foreigner's friends, enemies, and other circumstances so as to avoid offense to him and also to know where to find allies if necessary to mobilize against him, and so on.

6. Use the foreigner's own rules to control him, especially the Western legal concept of sovereignty, the idea that diplomats are accredited to governments (not to the local people), that domestic matters are beyond foreign question, and so on.

7. Stir the foreigner's conscience and sense of guilt so that he hamstrings himself.

8. Use some foreigners against others, to secure Chinese ends. Thus Chiang Kai-shek has cultivated American supporters of his own military doctrine, and by putting one third of his forces on Quemoy, with American help, he has made the defense of Quemoy probably necessary to the defense of Taiwan. Meanwhile Mao Tse-tung has found a staunch ally against Moscow in the state of Albania.

Behind these tactics, which are of course not really unique, lie certain traditional assumptions of Chinese politics that are rather different from our own:

1. China is a political and cultural universe. It cannot be divided. All Chinese belong to it.

2. There is only one Son of Heaven. He and his dynasty (or party) are the repository of final power. Popular consent is tacit.

3. Majority rule is mere mobocracy. Men are not equally endowed. The elite should rule. Hence plebiscites are unsound and insulting to dignity.

4. The ruler has a special virtue and prestige, which if maintained prolong his rule. Hence face is necessary to power holding, and criticism (as by a free press) is at once subversive.

5. Rule is personal. Law is not supreme, but a tool of administration. It is loyalty that supports a ruler. Hence civil rights must be limited and law subordinated to personal relations.

These ideas come down from the classic past. Many are out of date, unfeasible, and long since abandoned by modern-minded Chinese scholars and civil servants. Yet a certain residue remains and may be discerned today in Peking and also in Taipei, where, for example, an effort to start an independent loyal-opposition party, announced in June 1960, was met by the arrest of the chief leader, the publisher of *Free China Fortnightly,* Lei Chen, and his trial by a military court on utterly flimsy "sedition" charges. Lei was sentenced to ten years for publishing criticisms that would be considered perfectly normal and legitimate in a country which had freedom of speech and press. Subsequently Taipei's independent newspaper, *Kung Lun Pao,* which denounced this flagrant injustice, was taken over by the Kuomintang.

I mention these traditional diplomatic methods and these authoritarian political ideas not because they represent the best thought and practice of Free China today, but because they survive so strongly. Our ally Nationalist China is plainly a battleground between old and new, dictatorial and democratic, political concepts. This is to be expected. (The United States is similarly a battleground where the elementary idea of desegregation, for example, still produces rioting American mobs more violent than any to be seen in Taiwan.)

Indeed it is extraordinary that Taiwan does not suffer from more tension and disorder than it does. The Nationalist movement originated in the determination to recover China's sovereign rights and international dignity, after three thousand years of superiority over the known world had been turned upside down during a century of humiliation under the unequal treaties. Modern Chinese patriots, with this background, imbibed their full share of nationalistic ardor from the example of the nationalistic imperial powers. It was a proud day for Chiang Kai-shek when in 1943 he celebrated the final end of the unequal treaties and published his book, *China's Destiny,* to show the harm they had done to China. This celebration of the Kuomintang's final achievement of one of Sun Yat-sen's aims was no less poignant because by 1943, though foreign humiliation was being wiped out, domestic control of China was already almost lost to the Communists. After forty years of revolutionary success (in 1928), valiant resistance to attack (after 1937), victory (in 1945), rebellion, defeat, and exile (since 1949), the Kuomintang today carries a heavy burden of frustration, pride, and remorse. This history, and the emphasis it has given to militarism, may partly account for the Kuomintang's authoritarianism and its attack on free speech, which in any case underline the sharpness of the struggle between old and new in Taiwan.

For the United States these symptoms of political backwardness in Taipei raise the uncomforting question, is the ancient Chinese political tradition so strong and so authoritarian, and is the unity of all Chinese so precious, that

American ideas of an independent future for Taiwan in the non-Communist world are completely unrealistic?

Clearly, if we cannot get Chiang Kai-shek's part of China to join us in working toward political democracy, we will find it difficult indeed to live in the same world with Mao Tse-tung's China. More specifically, if we cannot even persuade Chiang to accept the independence of Taiwan, how can we persuade Mao to do so? This is precisely the dilemma which the Chinese political instinct has fashioned for us, creating out of weakness a strong bargaining position. We should recall that during World War II our aid to General Chiang was stimulated more than once by the fear that he might not be able to prevent his regime from collapsing and thus going over to the enemy.

Perhaps the answer to this problem is simply to overlook its existence for as long as possible. Why waste words in advocating a hated concept of Two Chinas (a misleading term which should be avoided on semantic grounds in any case), as long as our Seventh Fleet is able to patrol the Formosa Straits and use a Taiwan base? The fact of Taiwan's independence is our object, not the name.

Taiwan's recent history shows that we must pay more attention to the political aspect of our relations. In general, an increase of contact with late-modernizing areas is our best means of helping them in their political development. The American press has a role to play in Taiwan, whether the local press is free or muzzled. More contact with the great international world, so shrunken now by jet planes, can compensate for the smallness of an island home. Even though Taiwan may be small by Chinese standards, its thirteen millions would make it rank in size among the top third of the members of the United Nations.

It is by no means certain that an independent and also respectable Taiwan can be maintained, but we are obliged

63

to make the effort. To represent our political interest, however, no officer of the Foreign Service should be sent as ambassador to Taipei. The job requires a man of unconventional mold, uncommon sagacity, and incredible tenacity, a man with no worldly ambitions, no sense of haste, no hopes of personal success or fears of failure. He must have the utter confidence of the White House. He must also be as smart as the Chinese friends he will make.

Our ally Taiwan illustrates the truth which is beginning to dawn upon the American public, that our economic and military aid may be used by its recipients to bolster an antidemocratic kind of politics in allied countries. As Hans Morgenthau has put it, our quadruple fallacy has been to assume that dollars plus technological know-how equals economic development; economic development equals a stable society; a stable society equals democracy; and democracy equals peace. None of these assumptions being true, we must develop more specific programs of aid to political development abroad. Taiwan is a case in point.

Without going into more detail, perhaps I have indicated the very great difficulties we face in dealing with our Chinese allies, who are in many cases old friends, united with us in being anti-Communist and sufficiently dependent upon our assistance to be somewhat receptive to our views. We have differences in our strategic aims, personal interests, cultural values, and the like, but these are differences at least between allies, not enemies. How much greater therefore will be our problems in dealing with Communist China, a self-proclaimed enemy seventy times as big and intractable!

The dimensions of our Communist China problem are so great, their need for us as an "imperialist" enemy seems so permanent, that the China-America antagonism gives some promise of becoming the greatest tragedy of history, a contest of the Roman-Carthaginian type rather than a neighborly affair like those between Athens and Sparta, or France and Germany, or Japan and China.

Several factors may sustain an epochal antagonism between ourselves and mainland China. First, our opposed strategic positions, invincible sea-air power coming from across the Pacific opposed to unconquerable land power based in depth on the Chinese subcontinent. Second, our political aims in the world scene, we supporting an international order of one hundred-odd nation states under a United Nations structure, Peking maintaining a smaller-scale but more tightly organized world of its own based on the ancient continental Chinese culture area including China, Korea, Vietnam, Inner Asia, and some peripheral regions. This Chinese Communist bailiwick is only beginning to take shape, but the growing vigor of China's combined nationalistic-communistic drive is likely to make the area of Peking's influence increasingly distinct and in some ways autonomous.

Behind these factors of geopolitical strategy and power struggle lie two others, one economic, one cultural. Mainland China, once modernized, promises to be the poorest per capita of all modern countries. The population-resource balance in the Soviet Union is comparable to that in the United States, and it is feasible for the Soviets to aspire to emulate us in consumption, at least to some degree. The population-resource balance in China is far different and condemns the Chinese in perpetuity to a lower consumption level than mankind in other major states, except perhaps in India. China has begun her Communist-led industrialization with a population already far denser than Russia's, at a level of economic development far below Soviet Russia's starting point. China's unchecked and probably uncheckable population growth will leave her food supply always precarious. Whether her population is actually 700 million today, as generally assumed, or only 500 million, supposing we discount her so-called census of 1953 as merely another in the long series of ritualistic guesses indulged in by all Chinese dynasties, the fact remains that it will reach one billion unless a great catastrophe or an as yet unknown technique of birth control takes effect. A cereal diet, cloth shoes, cotton-padded clothing, crowded quarters, a mass life are in store for the Chinese people as far ahead as one can see. The private-automobile age, just dawning in Russia, will never reach China. It will remain a Spartan, embattled, have-not country, in which great public works, imposing monuments, and "socialist" achievements will have to substitute for personal material comforts even more than in the Soviet Union. Life will always be on a different material plane in China than in rich America, despite our own calamitous increase in numbers and in mass culture.

In turn this economic difference in consumption levels will tend to widen the great cultural gap between Chinese and Western or world civilization. As one travels through South and Southeast Asia one finds that the main cultural frontier lies not between Europe and Asia but between the rest of the world and the Chinese culture area, East Asia. This is partly because of the language barrier between the Chinese written characters and the alphabetic writing systems of other countries like Siam, Burma, and India. This literary dividing line is reinforced by the heritage of colonialism. South and Southeast Asian nations have had a direct contact with European countries which has left their legal systems, their urban intellectual life, their modern art and literature, for example, in the same world with European culture. At the same time, the Southeast Asian past is a bit less massive, multifaceted, and deep-rooted an influence on their modern life than is China's past on Chinese life. All in all, partly because of its sheer size, partly because of its long-continued tradition, partly because of its self-sufficient variety and richness of culture, Chinese civilization even in Communist garb bids fair to remain the one world area most distinctive from all other areas.

This distinctiveness of Chinese life was of course one cause of the century-long Sino-American love affair, an affair in which it now appears that the rich suitor from overseas was a good deal more ardent than the Chinese recipient of American attentions, whose cultural privacy was so rudely invaded. The gloomy prospect now is that this former attraction of opposites may for many years to come be transmuted by Communist manipulation into an antagonism. Casting Taiwan to the wolves and otherwise seeking to appease Peking's organized hostility is not likely to abate it, any more than appeasement ever does. International recognition and mutual contact, and the stark fact that mankind will now live or die together, are likely to be the best solvents of this hard crust of hatred for the United States that the Chinese Communists have built up to strengthen their domestic position.

Meanwhile, however, Peking's nuisance value in international life is steadily growing. Witness the thought being spread about that China is the one country that has no fear of nuclear war, since a loss of up to 300 million persons in each major country would leave China in top position to rebuild the world to its own satisfaction. This is nonsense, but it is an index of Chinese finesse in barbarian manipulation that Peking's professedly casual, couldn't-care-less attitude toward nuclear warfare seems to have succeeded in worrying both the United States and the Soviet Union.

In dealing with both Taiwan and mainland China our chief need is for intellectual resources. Our material resources are not inadequate, and we probably have enough

Americans overseas and a big enough apparatus of government and private agencies at work. The need now is far more competent personnel and more appropriate ideas of modern Asia and what to do about it. Intellectual development within the United States must take its place beside political development in allied countries overseas as our main agenda.

Intellectual development, of course, begins with language study. Too often it gets no further. Its main objective is a view of modern history and its problems in Asian terms, a view based on humanistic concerns as well as the social sciences, which takes full account of the Marxist-Leninist appeal to Asian intellectuals in search of certainty. Unless the non-Communist world can explain imperialism, landlordism, despotism, and low living standards better than the Communists, we cannot keep our intellectual frontier consonant with our political frontiers. As a rule of thumb it is safe to say that we will continue to lose ground until roughly half our specialists in Asia are specializing not in the transmission of Western technology but in the acquisition of learning about Asia. The modernization of Asia must be a two-way street. We Americans must radically change our own world view while we are in the process of helping Asian peoples to develop theirs. This applies particularly to our relations with the Chinese people. It underlies the opportunity, as yet largely unused, which we have in Taiwan.

In conclusion let me try to look critically at the perspectives suggested above. Must the Chinese communist attitude toward us continue indefinitely to be one of antagonism? By stressing different aspects of the historical record and appraising it more realistically, Peking could easily make us out to have been long-term, if sometimes misguided, friends of the Chinese people, as indeed we were. Is hostility inevitable?

The answer, I think, lies in the conditions of Chinese life and the nature of Communist totalitarianism. The latter is a system based somewhat less on faith, hope, and charity than on organized fear, suspicion, and hatred. The crowded condition of China, its poverty per capita and urgent need of order and industry, opened the way for totalitarianism in the first place. The same conditions seem likely to compel a continuance of the system, to keep the swelling population at work, fed, and under control. Not being able to dispense with despotism domestically, Communist China can hardly afford to drop foreign enemies from the outside horizon. Consequently the Leninist dogma of the capitalist-imperialist enemy rests not alone on its ideological merits, but is also called for by the hard conditions of Chinese life and government. Considering the remarkable unity and national effort that we, in our role of imperialist menace, have helped Peking to call forth from the Chinese people, it is hard to see how we could be more useful as friend or neutral than as long-term enemy.

In any case, our present power and wealth are combined with the happy American inexperience of those evils most other peoples have suffered. We are deficient in national suffering from feudal oppression, imperialist invasion, natural disaster, and civil strife (except for the Civil War, which as our one moment of agony still dominates the historical book-club trade). I suggest, in short, that for any people in deep trouble, like the Chinese, we happy Americans are likely to continue to be in ourselves a bit distasteful, if not actually hateful.

Finally, why should we expect our Chinese allies on Taiwan to go along indefinitely with our desire for a non-

Communist China where we can have contact and gain the other values I have outlined? Will Taiwan continue to be as enthusiastic as we are about the independence of Taiwan —sitting in an exposed position between power blocs, taunted as traitors from the mainland, and excluded from the massive show of national power and glory which Peking can offer to the world? After the present Taiwan leadership departs, why fight history? Ming loyalists held out on Quemoy Island and in Taiwan during most of forty years, from the 1640s to the 1680s. But a lost cause tends to die with its leaders. Why build American policy on remnants from a Chinese civil war, in the teeth of the rising nationalism and power of the world's largest state?

The answer is not clear-cut. It depends only partly on us. But before we let this question be oversimplified with the sentiment of irredentism, let us note certain facts. While the people in Taiwan are Chinese, so are most of the people of Singapore, and even of Hong Kong. The Chinese race is numerous and need not be all under one roof, any more than the Anglo-Saxons, the Slavs, or the Arabs. The Taiwanese proper have had fifty years under Japan, and many now look back to that period nostalgically. While today the two million mainlanders can still be distinguished from the native Taiwan Chinese, this will not always be so. In short, East and Southeast Asia have seen nine or ten new independent states emerge on the world scene in the last fifteen years. Among them Taiwan is one of the most stable, well developed, and potentially viable.

The question may still arise, am I not suggesting that the United States can use Taiwan to advantage? Do the Chinese in Taiwan want to be so used?

Utilization in this case seems to be mutual. I have suggested, for instance, that in the game of "who uses whom" in Sino-American relations since 1941, we Americans have been on balance the used more than the users. This inequality will probably continue. For those of our Chinese allies who are interested in political democracy, and there are a number, Taiwan can be a base and a laboratory, a fortunate opportunity, geographically arranged, to preserve and develop that finer part of the great Chinese heritage, the virtues of Confucian humanism, as opposed to the evils of the Legalist tyranny on the mainland. Taiwan may, with properly restrained and unsentimental aid, become a genuine beacon light for the hard-pressed Chinese people. This will remain a possibility, even though it is not certain anyone will succeed in realizing it.

An explicit definition of our motives, selfish and otherwise, is a step toward clarification of American policy. Americans still have a degree of zeal to convert the world, and we can build a policy more effectively on creative effort at growth than on conservatism and defense. Our China problem must be faced creatively, not in the terms of the past. To do this we need help from Taiwan, not to get us into war in a provocative defense of Quemoy, but to help us keep out of war through study of the grave problems we face in the Chinese quarter of the globe. The motives I have stressed may differ from those of Chiang Kai-shek (I believe they do), but it is wise to state such motives so that Americans may be more aware of what we seem to be trying to do in our aid to Taiwan. Seeing our own aims more clearly, we will be on more equal terms with our Chinese allies who, with their greater penetration of the human personality, perceive our aims already.

5 TAIWAN: MYTH,

DREAM, AND NIGHTMARE

The ambiguous status of Taiwan haunts American-Chinese relations; yet no major problem has been so continuously and carefully ignored in public. In Taiwan, three parties at interest—American, Nationalist Chinese, and Taiwanese Chinese—sleep in the same bed dreaming very different dreams. Whenever our China policy is unfrozen—if the United Nations, for example, should get Peking in—one man's dream in Taiwan may well turn out to be another man's nightmare.

The three parties are closely associated in the present government, but their *de facto* cooperation is possible only because the Nationalist make-believe is solemnly accepted by the Americans out of courtesy and expedience, and by the Taiwanese Chinese out of prudence under intimidation. Yet the palpable fact, that our ally the government of the Republic of China is based squarely upon a myth, does not ensure that its American and Taiwanese critics have any firmer grip on reality. American benevolence and Taiwanese nationalism may alike be frustrated unless the three parties get together constructively.

From *The New Republic*, February 5, 1966.

Of the three, the Nationalist position is of course best known. Since the Communist takeover of 1949, the government of the Republic of China has been temporarily confined to one of its provinces, the island of Taiwan, plus the fighting front, mainly on Quemoy Island in Amoy Harbor. The province of Taiwan, despite its growing tourist trade, is an embattled garrison state at war under martial law. The Nationalist government, still dominated by the Kuomintang and its leader, President Chiang Kai-shek, remains ready to counterattack and recover the mainland whenever that uncertain time arrives. Meanwhile it sits on top of the provincial government of Taiwan with skeleton staffs still designated to take over the other provinces once they are recovered. It thus sustains its constitutional structure as the government of China and vigorously maintains its international relations, occupying China's Security Council seat, keeping diplomatic relations with some fifty-seven countries (as compared with some fifty for the People's Republic of China in Peking), and sending technical-aid missions to African and other underdeveloped countries.

Obviously there is method in this myth. It not only gives the Nationalist or mainlander Chinese on Taiwan a sanction for dominating the island as well as a few thousand sinecure posts for faithful though aging Kuomintang officials. It also provides a worldwide rallying point for Chinese anti-Communist opposition to Peking. It keeps in being an armed rival for power; China's civil war is not yet over; Chairman Mao Tse-tung, it is hoped, cannot yet sleep well at night. Indeed, if Peking-Washington relations deteriorate into open warfare, President Chiang may well feel his posture has been justified by events.

The Americans, on their part, have not wanted to take responsibility for dismantling the Nationalist myth and damaging the government. Chiang Kai-shek knows his sovereign rights. Hypercritical diplomats who insist that the "king has no clothes" can be labeled unfriendly and wanting in tact. Free China can still perhaps be made a partisan issue in American politics. After all, Chiang is in charge, the economy is developing (so well that American aid has ceased), and we need access to a Chinese area that is non-Communist, where intelligence work, military programs, language training, and academic research can all be carried on. The Nationalists include many men of talent, many trained in the United States, skilled administrators, dedicated scholars, people oriented toward the West. We need such Chinese allies.

In the last analysis, the Americans have not wanted to push an ally around. Our aid has buttressed the Nationalist government domestically, but we have not wanted to intervene in Taiwan's domestic politics. We believe in self-determination, the main sanction we claim for our effort in Vietnam. We don't want to try to mastermind Chinese politics.

Just at this point, however, the American dream for Taiwan diverges from the Nationalist myth. Instinctively (to say nothing of our 1954 treaty obligation) we feel we cannot let two million mainlanders and eleven million Taiwanese be taken over by Peking against their will. The Taiwan living standard is far higher than on the continent. Neither Kuomintang refugees nor the Taiwan populace can be surrendered to Communist control unless, which seems unthinkable, they solemnly vote by secret ballot in favor of it. Thus the latent American sentiment is for the continued independence of Taiwan on the basis of self-determination. This makes sense in the American political vocabulary, but not in the Nationalist.

The Taiwanese interest is represented by an independence movement, but it seems to lack much organization or overt following. Its past and future are probably more substantial than its present manifestations. It stems from three basic facts: (1) Taiwan is not ancient China but through Chinese migration was settled as recently as were the thirteen colonies in America—a very recent event, in the long perspective of Chinese history. (2) Before Chinese nationalism had arisen, Taiwan was modernized as a Japanese colony; during the half century from 1895 to 1945 it acquired an economic-technological base superior to that of continental China. (3) Finally, the Nationalist takeover of 1945 ended in the great Taiwanese protest of February 1947 and the ensuing Nationalist crackdown and massacre.

This grim story is detailed for the first time by eyewitnesses in *Formosa Betrayed* by George Kerr. His itemized record of organized Chinese official looting of both the public and private sectors is macabre and hair-raising. The United States kept hands off, while rapacious Nationalists despoiled Taiwan as conquered territory. This systematic exploitation by carpetbagging officials built to a climax in the eventual Taiwanese protest of 1947 and the systematic Nationalist execution of thousands, which wiped out a whole generation of Taiwan's potential leadership.

This holocaust, of course, preceded the arrival of most of the mainlanders in 1949. It did not commend them to the Taiwanese survivors, who had been liberated from Japan's ruthless efficiency only in time to long for its return. The subsequent success of the Nationalist land reform and economic development with American aid have grown tissue over the scar. But the sense of Taiwanese or "Formosan" national identity is still expressed by refugee groups in Tokyo, even though its expression is kept down by the police and the widespread informer network on the island.

The dream of "Taiwan for the Taiwanese" in one sense is being realized by time. College freshmen today are likely to be Taiwan-born even when of mainlander parents. Taiwanese already form a majority of army privates and a sizable part of the remodeled Kuomintang and local administration. The mainlander-Taiwanese antagonism might die away, and the American good will toward smaller states struggling for "independence" might have full opportunity, if the myth that Taiwan is China could be given up. But can it be?

The answer is uncertain, for China is a far country, with a political tradition already 1,400 years old at the time of the Magna Carta and a sense of pride commensurate with its age. China's ancient ethnocentrism is only heightened by modern nationalism, both in Peking and in Taipei. Look at the record. Chiang and Mao, though deadly rivals, agree that there is only one Chinese realm. Since 200 B.C. it has embraced all the Sons of Han in a single entity. Occasionally it has been divided, only to be reunited bigger and stronger than ever. It is coterminous with Chinese culture. It includes peripheral peoples like the Miao and Chuang tribes, Tibetans, Uighur Turks, or Mongols. They are entitled not to "self-determination" but only to "autonomy" (*tzu-chih*, self-government) within the Chinese realm. In practice, this now means Sinicization, though in periods of weakness it has meant no more than a Chinese claim to ultimate overlordship.

Recognition of the independence of Taiwan as a state is thus an idea thinkable only by Taiwanese or by non-Chinese who are "anti-Chinese." Labeled (quite inaccurately) the Two Chinas Policy, this concept is anathema to Peking and Taipei alike. One hesitates even to put it in print. Though second nature to most Americans, it is evil to *all* Chinese, except the powerless Taiwanese underground. Here is a real cultural-political confrontation. It is not just an old man's crotchet.

The unity of all Chinese in the realm of "all under Heaven" has been the focus of Chinese politics from the most ancient times. Chiang Kai-shek entered history as the architect of the Northern Expedition of 1926, devoted to the reunification of China as the first step in its national regeneration. This is an idea far grander than that of a Cavour, a Bismarck, or a Masaryk. Where European nationalists have built nations, rulers of modern China have had to remake an entire society and culture, unique in both size and age. The Son of Heaven was more many-sided than any Western potentate. His successors, contenders for central power in China, have needed a special strength to take on an especially stupendous task.

The role of a Chinese unifier is well chiseled in history: he leads by courage, character, and determination. Loyal to followers, implacable to foes, he remains unaffected by the blows of fate. He never surrenders. His life he may lose, but not his dignity. In this stubborn mold, President Chiang still claims the Mandate of Heaven to rule all China.

This explains why the political process, like political thinking, remains frozen on the island. The Nationalist government, a higher echelon above the Taiwan provincial government, cannot be changed or controlled by Taiwan politics. Even though the dominant Kuomintang has in fact permitted independent Taiwanese candidates to run for office and some have defeated KMT candidates, the door is still not open for organized political opposition.

Behind this rigidity lies a basic tenet of Chinese politics —that a leader holds power by virtue of his conduct, which includes his policies. His institutional function as power holder cannot be distinguished from his personal exercise of power. For this reason our concept of a loyal opposition is not in the Chinese style. Criticism of the ruler in the old days was largely reserved for official censors, who criticized within channels and at their peril. Latter-day Sons of Heaven like Ngo Dinh Diem have not suffered opposition gladly. Neither does Chiang Kai-shek. Any real opposition to his policies cuts at the base of his prestige and therefore of his power. Thus the Taiwanese electorate cannot be sovereign in Taiwan.

If our differences with our Taiwan ally in political values and methods are objectively recognized, rather than papered over by the manipulations of public relations, we shall be better prepared to face Peking together. We must recognize that we do not all dream the same dream. The American interest is to preserve the substance of Taiwan's independence without demanding that our cherished English-language formula of "self-determination" be accepted in Chinese terminology. Let us continue to leave the Seventh Fleet in the Formosa Straits and the Taiwan-China relationship ambiguous and not demand neat definitions.

Is there any in-between formula that could somehow reconcile the American and Taiwanese impulses toward self-determination and the instinctive Nationalist demand for the unity of all Chinese? The only formula available from history has a distinctly imperialist flavor, derived from great power deals of half a century ago. By this imperialist precedent, Taiwan's independence could be called "autonomy," the way the *de facto* independence of Tibet and Mongolia was labeled after 1915. The Chinese empire had fallen apart, and Britain and Russia recognized the autonomy of Tibet and Outer Mongolia, respectively, while China continued to claim suzerainty over both areas. Under this formula, Taiwan's separation from the continent could be viewed in the long sweep of Chinese history as purely temporary, a matter of only a few decades or at most a mere century or two. Independent Tibet, as it turned out, did not survive long after Britain left India, though it is still called autonomous; but Outer Mongolia did survive, with Soviet backing, and is now a UN member. From "autonomy" one could move either way. But both Peking and Taipei will denounce the idea as "two Chinas." We should avoid that term and call it "dual representation." Like the Soviet Union, which has three votes in the UN Assembly, China would have two.

PART III

COMMUNIST CHINA AND AMERICAN POLICY

6 EDGAR SNOW

IN RED CHINA

Edgar Snow was the first journalist to get into the small northwest area known as Red China in 1936 and give the story of Mao Tse-tung and his followers to the outside world. *Red Star over China,* published in 1937, became a classic, read everywhere for its biography of Mao, its account of guerrilla tactics, its prognosis of the trend of China's revolution. Twenty-five years later Snow discovered Red China all over again. In 1960 he spent five months touring the country, the first American reporter who had been there in the old days to do so, and thus he can give us before-and-after comparisons. *The Other Side of the River* makes effective use of his background knowledge of Red China. It is a bit as if Marco Polo were playing Rip van Winkle.

Like any major work on a great and controversial problem, *The Other Side of the River* gives the inquiring reader homework to do on many problems of attitude and judgment. The book is full of vivid firsthand detail, personal insights, and not a little philosophizing about the condition of mankind. What lies behind it? What were the author's assumptions and sensitivities, his aims and oppor-

From *The Atlantic Monthly,* January 1963.

tunities? How far did he penetrate the mainland scene? How can American readers evaluate (taking into account their own personal and perhaps barely conscious attitudes concerning Red China) Snow's attitude and experience, and the various attitudes of the Chinese whom he saw, from old friends among the leadership to young party activists and peasants in villages? What realities of China today filter through all these layers of feeling and interpretation?

Leaving aside the embarrassing question whether it is feasible to generalize about 700 million people, as we daily try to do, we can look first at the author, then at his book, and through it, if possible, at China in 1960.

When Edgar Snow became a journalist on J. B. Powell's *China Weekly Review* in Shanghai in 1928, he was twenty-two years old, fresh from Kansas City, on his way, as he thought, around the world. By the time he got into Red China in 1936, he had had seven years' experience of the treaty ports, the great northwest famine of 1929–1930, the Japanese undeclared war of 1931–1932 (which he reported in *Far Eastern Front*), and student movements at Yenching University outside Peiping. Like so many Westerners, he had become an intimately involved and yet immune spectator of Chinese life and its intricate daily struggles, especially the absorbing intensity of personal and political relations in a society where the individual must rely not on impersonal institutions, but on other people. By the time Mao Tse-tung, Chu Teh, Chou En-lai, and the other Communist leaders had completed their hegira, the Long March, escaping from central China to the northwest, and were ready to tell the story of their struggle, Ed Snow at the age of thirty was prepared to understand its implications and report it in very human terms.

Red Star over China made him, more than most successful journalists, a sort of institution, an interpreter of the

Chinese Communist revolution. Some critics felt that without him it might never have occurred, or at least not gained so much attention. After the united front of 1937–1940 fell apart, he left China, though not before he had helped found the Chinese Industrial Cooperatives movement and seen the Red areas again in their wartime expansion. In 1941 Snow prophesied in *The Battle for Asia* that "liberals who build up hopes that the Communists of China are 'different' and 'only reformers' and have abandoned revolutionary methods . . . are doomed to ultimate disillusionment."

As a *Saturday Evening Post* correspondent, he saw wartime Russia and India, postwar Europe, Japan, and Korea, yet he remained a China hand in the common meaning of the term—he had left a bit of his heart there. Snow's career and opinions are so fully on record, surveyed also in his autobiography, *Journey to the Beginning* (1958), that he is a fairly definite quantity. He is sympathetic to the domestic human aspirations of revolution, unresponsive to its ideological dogma, and has the advantage of thirty years' perspective on the hard conditions of Chinese life.

Getting back to Peking, as the first experienced American journalist in a decade, was not easy. The State Department, Snow says, tried its very best to dissuade *Look* magazine from sending him. His sharpest strictures are applied to the State Department's obstruction of journalists' going to China. He believes Peking welcomed him in 1960 partly because as early as 1949 he had prophesied Communist China's independence of Moscow, and accordingly he had been banned from Russia during Stalin's lifetime. Apparently the Sino-Soviet rift had widened enough to let him in.

Many old friends met him at the Peking airport. In five months, from July to November 1960, he visited nineteen cities in fourteen provinces, had seventy-odd interviews with all kinds of people—no lack of "opportunity to *see* China," despite the usual limitations on a foreign reporter, traveling with guides and usually interviewing through interpreters. He found all-wave radios sold everywhere and available in most hotel rooms. He roamed Peking alone with a camera and brought out all his films uncensored. "Chinese security is built into the society," he explains at length; the whole community is trained to check on all its members.

In addition to all the sights, inspections, receptions, and briefings, Snow spent a total of about twelve hours conversing with Premier Chou En-lai, ate with Chairman Mao in his home, and spent some nine hours interviewing him. He also caught up with the life histories of a multitude of people he had known before. All this makes a big book in eighty-six short chapters.

The Other Side of the River gets its title from Pascal: "A strange justice that is bounded by a river! Can anything be more ridiculous than that a man should have the right to kill me because he lives on the other side." This expression of the present-day human dilemma, how to avoid organized killing while maintaining differently organized societies, indicates Snow's rather nonideological, humanitarian view: Communist China exists, we all have to coexist. Caught between opposed societies, he is in the usual area specialist's dilemma—how to bridge the Pacific in meaningful terms. His Chinese hosts wanted him to transmit their sense of historical grievance and proud accomplishment. American readers may want him to evaluate Red China in a few well-chosen words, pro or con. Both may be frustrated. Snow is neither an inexperienced traveler susceptible to the sheer enthusiasm of a fellow traveler nor a Kremlinologist chiefly devoted to analyzing power relations as betrayed in Communist jargon. A field reporter, he tries to avoid the oversimplicity of the library researcher, who deals only with documents, not people, or of the columnist, who has to know what he thinks in the first place. His first-person narrative is a mixture of conversations, epitomes of history, reminiscent personal flashbacks, analyses of institutions, and comments on policy. When the party faithful tell him: This road was only a mule track before Liberation, Snow can reply: That's strange, I rode a truck over it in 1939.

No other volume on Communist China has covered so broad a range with so much perception. Nevertheless, "travel in China," says Snow, "provides no magic bag of answers." To make it more difficult, the returning traveler confronts at home an "amazing number of things people know about China which just aren't so"—for example, widespread starvation, of which he could find no evidence in 1960. "They were all dying," he says, "but apparently only at about the same rate people are dying everywhere."

The main impact of *The Other Side of the River* lies, I think, in its indication of how dangerously wide the river really is. On the American side there is stereotyped ignorance, due less to lack of data than to lack of comparable experience. For America "to accept the Chinese revolution requires too big an act of imagination from a country that has not suffered, itself, for nearly a hundred years."

On the Chinese side there is, first of all, the arrogant doctrinaire and puritanical zeal of the revolution, now implanted in so many sincere and devoted patriotic youths. Snow found Chinese soldiers, for instance, obviously shocked at the idea of premarital sexual relations and baffled by the concept of being a conscientous objector. He found that enthusiastic schoolgirls who were eager to quote Chairman Mao were otherwise uninformed and uninstructed about the outside world.

In recording his conversations with Chinese young and old, Snow continually assesses their lives in their terms and in our terms, and tries looking at "imperialist" America and Communist China through their eyes as well as ours. Many of these exchanges take on a wry sense of irony. He soon learns to anticipate the cliché. "I knew what was coming next and silently joined him in chorus . . . 'nothing against the American people, it's only American imperialism.' "

In general, the industrial and agricultural development, spurred on by the zeal of the revolution, seemed truly enormous, "much greater than I had expected to find." Similarly, the breakup of the statistical system, which contributed to the economic collapse after the Great Leap Forward of 1958, was due in part to overzealous statistical reporting, with "politics in command." That the revolutionary ardor overreached itself in 1958 was partly Mao's responsibility.

As to Mao's view of the world, Snow feels "his grasp of the Western world is a schematic one based on methods of Marxist analysis of classes as they exist in backward economies like the one he grew up in. He lacks sufficient understanding of the subtle changes brought about in those classes in advanced 'welfare states' by two hundred years of the kind of transformation China is only now entering." These out-of-date assumptions as to Western realities are reinforced by lack of contact. "Mao was never out of China until . . . 1949. He has never seen any non-Communist foreign land, not even India or Japan. . . . Up to 1962, only one person in the Politburo, Lo Fu, had ever seen any part of the New World."

Snow cannot forget that the American leadership is in an equal position of ignorance. It has never seen the new China, but seems content to rely on intelligence which is necessarily collected and filtered for security purposes. Returning after his marathon talk with Mao, he was invited to the State Department for an interview which lasted only ten minutes. "It shocked me that the American instrument to whom Mao Tse-tung had bothered to talk for nine hours —obviously with the expectation that he might reach an ear in the White House—could be so completely wasted." Snow believes that the mutual Sino-American ignorance is mutually maintained.

His experience of both sides leaves him a liberal in his views, and liberal with criticism. The book winds up with several broad surveys of cold-war areas that seek to ascertain a method whereby opposing interests might possibly be reconciled. However much one may agree or disagree with this individual view, its contribution lies in the bifocal effort to comprehend both sides in emotional as well as rational terms, an effort which is seldom really made on either side, since all observers have been staying on one side of the river, loyal and ignorant, dutifully responsive to the strategic and abstract considerations of their national interest, quite unable to respond to the human goodwill which is usually felt on the personal level by the distant "enemy." This all but fatal estrangement of peoples, in a world now so shrunk by technology, can be overcome only by the peoples themselves, by an "alert and knowledgeable citizenry" capable of recognizing that as a race "we do stand at the threshold of Childhood's end."

Snow's conclusion bears a typical optimism which a more pessimistic historian may question. The Sino-American estrangement has grown up since the 1920s, when China's revolution first entered the villages and began to take on national forms quite alien to the prosperous, legal-minded, individualistic American tradition. Snow's caustic criticisms of various aspects of the United States reflect partly the frustrations of a whole generation of Americans interested in China who have seen many liberal dreams fade and the Sino-American divergence steadily widen. Just at the time in the 1940s when Communism seemed to Americans in the United States to become their mortal enemy, it seemed to the Chinese people in China to become their savior. Ever since, the national life of each people has been oriented against the other. The Sino-American antagonism, like the Sino-Soviet, comes from the deep-seated conflict of national interests, values, and attitudes.

How to resolve the Soviet-American conflict rightly preoccupies us. Since the Soviets developed their missiles, we have built up a considerable program of diplomatic contact and cultural exchange. This contact seems helpful to us in avoiding a disastrous Soviet-American conflict. With Communist China we have already fought once, in Korea, but we still avoid the kind of journalistic, academic, and cultural contact we have with the Soviets.

In the absence of contact during the last thirteen years, ignorance and self-righteousness have increased on both sides of the river. They can lead only toward further conflict.

7 NEW THINKING

ABOUT CHINA

For more than a decade we have avoided looking at our China problem, hoping it would go away. But it is still there, waiting to be faced. To understand it, we need historical perspective on China, on ourselves, and on our relations.

In the dozen years since McCarthy tried to turn the lights out, academic study of China has gone ahead, but the State Department has groped along without the help of those purged Foreign Service officers whose firsthand experience in China would have provided useful insight. New talent is emerging, but it is still junior and never knew Peking.

The new American look at China, now under way seventeen years after the Communist takeover, begins with several facts. Contrary to John Foster Dulles' official hopes of 1959, Chairman Mao's revolution will not soon pass away, even though Mao will. We are preparing to live with it, as we now live with the Soviet revolution. Our cold-war policy of "containment and isolation" of China is shifting, in A. Doak Barnett's phrase, to one of "containment but not isolation," toward a better balance.

From *The Atlantic Monthly,* June 1966; based on testimony before the Senate Committee on Foreign Relations, March 10, 1966.

Yet it takes two to de-isolate. Peking's price for an end of fighting in Asia seems likely to be exorbitant; contact will come only slowly and with pain; and a return of anything like Sino-American "friendship" seems quite out of the question.

Now that the blinders are off and our China policy is back under public scrutiny, we see new actors in a new confrontation. Peking is no longer part of Moscow's monolith. Nuclear-armed China is becoming a great power, a maker or destroyer of world stability. The Chinese, while verbally bellicose and threatening the world with revolutionary takeover, have in fact kept almost all their troops at home, while the generous Americans, seeking international stability, have sent large forces to fight close to China in Vietnam. We need to apply fresh perspective to both sides.

Down to the nineteenth century, China was its own world, an enormous, ancient, isolated, unified, and self-sufficient empire stretching from the latitude of Hudson Bay to Cuba, or from the Baltic Sea to the Sahara Desert. It had a great deal of domestic commerce to meet its needs, but was cut off from Western Asia by the high mountains and deserts of Central Asia and thus remained isolated throughout most of its history. So it preserved a continuity of development in the same area over some three or four thousand years, and had a strong tendency to look inward. Non-Chinese were peripheral and inferior.

The Chinese did not believe in the equality of all men, which was obviously untrue. They believed in selecting an elite of talent, training these men in the classical orthodoxy, and promoting them as officials to keep the populace under control and maintain the system. We need not labor the point that China today still has a ruling class of people selected for their abilities, who propagate a true teaching under a sage ruler and strive to keep the various social classes in order.

The long record of Chinese foreign relations shows the importance attached to the political myths of China's superiority and rule by virtue. Maintaining this ideological orthodoxy in written form helped the emperor keep power in fact, because the recorded "facts" always sustained the theory. It was like the advertisement for paint—"Save the surface [or the record] and you save all."

The emperors were constantly spelling out the true doctrines, having them read in the Confucian temples and studied by all scholars. Heterodoxy and deviation could not be permitted or, if they did exist, could not be acknowledged to exist. The emperor's asserted supremacy over all mankind was the foundation of state power. Consequently, the monarchy's gradual failure and eventual extinction in 1912 were an epochal calamity.

Even when the foreigners became more powerful, the myth of China's superiority had to be solemnly recorded and preserved in ritual. This stress on orthodoxy strikes one today, when Peking is continuing its nationwide indoctrination in Chairman Mao's true teachings. Orthodoxy seems more necessary than ever to keep in order the world's most numerous citizenry.

The disaster that hit China in the nineteenth century is one of the most comprehensive any people has ever experienced. The ancient tradition of China's superiority, plus this modern phase of disaster, undoubtedly produced one first-class case of frustration. It could not seem right that a civilization once at the top should be brought so low. The nineteenth-century disaster began with a great population increase during the peaceful eighteenth century, a consequent weakening of administrative efficiency, and maybe some popular demoralization, evident in the beginning of opium smoking. In the Opium War the Chinese were fighting against the opium trade, conducted by both foreigners and Chinese, while the British were fighting, in the broad sense, against the tribute system, demanding that China drop its claim to superiority and join the modern international trading world, the same thing we are waiting for today more than a century later.

The Opium War and the unequal treaties of the 1840s gave our merchants and missionaries a privileged status as agents of Westernization in the Chinese treaty ports. Throughout the following century, Western influence gradually disintegrated the old Chinese civilization. As the disaster gained momentum, Western gunboats proved that China had to acquire modern arms and scientific technology, and then had to have Western industries, for which it was necessary to have Western learning, and eventually Western institutions and even a Western type of government. The omnipotent monarchy was humbled. The prestige of the Confucian classics evaporated. The Confucian type of family structure began to crack. China's superiority vanished, even culturally.

The generation of Chinese that lived through this long-continued upheaval, which happened in our grandfathers' time, experienced a deepening crisis. The sacred values of proper conduct and social order proved useless. The ancient faith in China's superiority as a civilization was slowly strangled. The privileged foreigners came in everywhere and gradually stirred up a Chinese nationalism.

So complete was the disaster that in the twentieth century a new order has had to be built from the ground up. Western doctrines of all kinds were tried out between the 1890s and the 1930s. The thing that proved effective was the Leninist type of party dictatorship, an elite recruited under discipline according to a new orthodoxy, organized something like an old Chinese secret society, united in the effort to seize power and re-create a strong state. This nationalistic aim, represented first by the Kuomintang, overrode every other consideration. The kind of Western individualism propagated by our missionaries had little chance in the midst of the political struggle to rebuild a strong state, and even less chance after Japanese aggression began in 1931.

In their retrospective humiliation and sense of grievance over the enormous disaster of the nineteenth century, modern Chinese have generally felt that their country was victimized. So it was—by fate. Circumstance has made China the worst accident case in history.

But the Chinese view of history for reasons already mentioned has always been very personal, seeing rulers rise or fall by their good or bad conduct. To attribute China's modern fate to a historical abstraction like "cultural homeostasis" (that is, China had developed so much self-equilibrating stability that it did not respond quickly to the Western threat) is not emotionally satisfying to Chinese patriots. It is like asking a man run over by a truck to blame it on a congested traffic pattern. He will say, No, it was a truck. Consequently, Chinese of all camps have united in denouncing the obvious aggressions of the foreign powers. Marxism-Leninism caught on in the 1920s, even though the proletariat was minuscule and class struggle minimal, by offering its devil theory to explain China's modern foreign relations: "Capitalist imperialism" from abroad combined with "feudal reaction" at home to attack, betray, and exploit the Chinese people and distort their otherwise normal development toward "capitalism" and "socialism." Thus a great Communist myth of imperialist victimization has become the new national myth of a revived central power at Peking.

Those who see Communist ideology as an all-conquering virus may prefer to discount history and omit it from their diagnosis. But to understand China without history, to divorce this most historical-minded of all cultures from its past, is quite impossible. The Chinese Communists themselves use history to "prove" their anti-imperialist doctrine. Communist ideology and China's historical record thus overlap.

One can easily see the utility of having American imperialism (as distinct from the American "people," who are somehow "exploited" by Wall Street) as China's national enemy: our eternal menace justifies Peking's draconian rule. One wonders if the Chinese Communist Party could survive without us; our role as enemy seems essential to Chairman Mao's morality play. Yet we must recognize there is more to it than theory and propaganda. Lenin's picture of economic imperialism has been broadened by Mao to include all foreign contact. Even missionary good works are now seen to have been "cultural imperialism." The latent feeling is one of resentment against the whole great fact of China's having fallen behind the modern outside world.

If we now turn to look at ourselves, we can see where American self-esteem and resentment come into play, for we are generally conscious of having long befriended China and recently been kicked in the teeth for it. We can only dimly imagine how the proud Chinese elite has suffered from being on the receiving end of modernization.

Being on the giving end of modernization ourselves, in the privileged status thrust upon us by the treaty system, most of us enjoyed our contact with China. We could be upper-class foreigners commanding servants and riding in rickshaws while still remaining egalitarian grass-roots democrats in our own conscience. The Chinese were polite, and countless Americans made warm friends among them. The American people built up a genuine, though sometimes patronizing, fondness for "China." Unfortunately, this now turns out to have been an unrealistic and naive attitude. The Americans were conscious of their own good intentions and less conscious of the humiliation that their superior circumstances often inflicted upon their Chinese friends.

When Britain and others fought their colonial wars, the Americans enjoyed the fruits of aggression without the moral responsibility. By 1900 the British, the French, and the Japanese had fought wars with China; the Russians had seized territory; and all of them, as well as the Germans, had seized special privileges in spheres of influence.

The Americans had done none of these things and came up instead with the Open Door doctrine, which soon expanded to include not only the open door for trade but also the idea of China's integrity as a nation. Thus we Americans could pride ourselves on championing China's modernization and self-determination. We considered ourselves above the nasty imperialism and power politics of the Europeans. We developed a self-image of moral superiority. The Open Door and benevolence toward Chinese nationalism became the basis of our Far Eastern policy until war with Japan brought us up against the realities of power politics. Then we began to realize, for almost the first time, that the power structure of East Asian politics had been held together by the British Navy in the nineteenth century, and by the British and Japanese navies under the Anglo-Japanese Alliance from 1902 to 1922.

Today we find ourselves in an onerous situation trying to maintain the power balance in East Asia. Vietnam is reminiscent in some ways of the colonial wars of the nineteenth century, a type of situation we generally succeeded in avoiding in that era. I do not contend that we today are simply nineteenth-century imperialists come back to life, but I do not believe we can escape our historical heritage entirely, any more than Mao can. We have been part and parcel of the long-term Western approach to Asia and ought to see ourselves in that perspective. The Western powers have played major roles in East and Southeast Asia for four hundred years even if we have not. The West has made its contribution while also precipitating the nationalist revolutions. American merchants and missionaries joined in making this Western contribution. We cannot now condemn and disown the old British Empire, for instance, just because we let the British fight the dirty colonial wars while we got the benefits. We were and are involved in East Asian power politics at least as much as in those of Europe. But Vietnam today gives us a more severe crisis of moral conscience partly because during most of our history we have felt morally superior to the imperialist powers.

Stuck in a dirty war today, we would do well to lower our self-estem, not be so proud, acknowledge our Western inheritance of both good and evil, and see ourselves as hardly more noble and not much smarter than the British and French in their day. We cannot take East Asia *or* ourselves out of power politics.

Once we see ourselves as an integral part, and now the major representative, of the Western world that was the nineteenth-century agent of traditional China's downfall, perhaps we can reduce our own resentment at Mao's resentment.

Given these cognate Sino-American resentments on either side—and each has a long list of grievances, too long even to suggest here—what can we expect in our future relations? First, we can be sure that a resumption of American generosity to China will not cure but only worsen our mutual enmity. "Let us recognize them and get it over with," as some put it, is not a psychologically feasible approach. Neither is giving them grain, like the famine relief of old, for it puts China back on the short end of things, receiving our beneficence. Instead, we should take the long way around and expect our own relations with China to improve only after others' relations have done so. We should lower the level of polemics if we can, but not anticipate a direct reconciliation.

This suggests, in the second place, that we can hardly take the lead, but instead should acquiesce in the effort to get Peking to participate in the international order rather than try to subvert and destroy it. This is primarily a psychological problem for the international community to deal with. Therapy for Peking's present almost paranoid state of mind must follow the usual lines of therapy: it must lead the rulers of China gradually into different channels of experience until by degrees they reshape their picture of the world and their place in it. This program should get Peking into a multitude of activities abroad. China should be included in all international conferences, as on disarmament, and in international associations, both professional and functional; in international sports, not just ping-pong; and in exchange of news, technology, persons, and trade with everyone, including ourselves, except for strategic goods. One thinks naturally of the UN agencies and participation in the Security Council as well as the Assembly. Yet all this can come only step by step, with altercation all along the way—not an easy process but at least a political one, more constructive than warfare.

The remolding of Chairman Mao, the greatest remolder of others in history, is not something outsiders can attempt. But he and his colleagues are great believers in tactical shifts to meet changing circumstances. Their militant ideals may remain out of reach, but changed tactics can lead them into that great coolant of expansionism: coexistence.

In accepting the international world as an alternative to trying to subvert it, Chinese behavior can meet China's needs. One of these is the craving for greater prestige in the world to redress the balance of the last century's humiliations. For China to be in the center of the world's councils seems to any Chinese patriot only right and proper. The Peking government also needs prestige to maintain itself domestically. In addition, like all developing countries, China needs certain kinds of aid through exchanges of technology, of persons, and of goods.

The international community can also expect Peking to respond sooner or later to the opportunity to manipulate foreigners against one another. This traditional way of dealing with outsiders can be attempted in any conclave like the United Nations. But others also play the game; in fact, it is the essence of diplomacy. As all these motives come into play, Peking will become more involved in bilateral relationships and be influenced by others whose desire is for peace rather than violence. In the end, after much travail, all this may make coexistence more attractive. Yet in the meantime, Peking's subversive efforts to foment "people's wars of liberation" may be expected to continue and will have to be countered.

Thus a new American attitude can catalyze rather than obstruct the stabilizing of Peking's relations with the international world. It is time to shift from trying to isolate Peking, which only worsens our problem, to a less exposed position where we can acquiesce in the growth of contact between Peking and other countries and let *them* suffer the impact of Peking's abrasiveness.

Similarly, concerning Taiwan, we cannot demand that our sovereign ally Chiang Kai-shek pension off his aging Nationalist government echelons and build up the elected Taiwan provincial government to run the island, thus acknowledging defeat in China's civil war. Such steps must be left for his successors. But meantime, the Seventh Fleet can continue to quarantine the Formosa Straits, and we can advocate "self-determination" though we cannot enforce it. In the end we shall have to let Taipei and Peking work out their respective United Nations relationships. We cannot do it for them.

But this helping to open the door for China's participation in the world scene is only one part of an American policy. The other part is to hold the line, for the Chinese are no more amenable to pure sweetness and light than other revolutionaries. Encouraging them to participate in the United Nations and other parts of the growing international order has to be combined with a cognate attitude of firmness backed by force. Military containment on the Korean border, in the Formosa Straits, and somehow in Vietnam cannot soon be abandoned.

Indeed, the new effort at nonmilitary contact with Peking, here advocated, is feasible in American policy precisely because we are being so active militarily in Vietnam. Contact and negotiation, far from being an either-or alternative to fighting, are essential to balance our continued military presence and keep it within a larger, political framework. If military containment is not to trigger major war, it must be explicitly and credibly limited, not subject to open-ended escalation. "Containment" should aim simply to contain, not to terrify, confuse, or, least of all, provoke. Recognition of military strength on both sides, and also its limitations on both sides, is an inducement to stabilizing relations—particularly if it is recognized that

101

China is a land animal, unconquerable at home, while the United States is a sea-and-air animal, able to frustrate the Maoist type of revolutionary takeover abroad but not to take over itself.

Containment alone is a dead-end street, but a policy of contact works in both directions. Both sides give and both get. Who can doubt that our own militancy was defused, from the level of unreasoning fear down to the level of political competition, when Nikita Khrushchev became an American TV personality? What might not Chou En-lai's black eyebrows accomplish? The Chinese instinct for diplomacy will soon find that in the United States there is some sort of audience responsive to every view, but our major sentiments of goodwill respond less to dogma and bombast than to reasoned self-interest and give-and-take. Thus a program of contact is a two-way street.

The first step is the hardest, for it must be taken in our own thinking—to abandon both the fear of Chinese military menace and the hope of Chinese friendliness. China will not fight us unless we get too close to its frontiers and ask for trouble. The Chinese will not respond to friendly overtures except to repeat "Get out of Taiwan," which by our own principles we will not do unless genuinely asked by the people there. Peking will continue to damn us for crimes we did not commit and evil aims we do not have.

In short, my reading of history is that Peking's rulers now shout aggressively out of manifold frustrations, that isolation intensifies their ailment and makes it self-perpetuating, and that international contact with China on many fronts can open a less warlike chapter in its foreign relations. But we are dealing with revolutionists who face enormous domestic difficulties, labor under serious emotional problems themselves, and have a warped understanding of the outside world. In facing reality, to avoid disaster we must understand their dilemma as well as our own.

8 WHY PEKING CASTS

US AS THE VILLAIN

A growing number of United States senators, headed by
Edward M. Kennedy and George McGovern, have been
suggesting the appointment of a panel to review American
policy toward China. Reviving this discussion is certainly
desirable and indeed long overdue. Yet it has its dangers—
things taken out of the deep freeze deteriorate if nothing
further is done to them. Any attempt to resume our tradi-
tionally generous attitude toward the Chinese people, for
example, will encounter disheartening hostility. The Chinese Communist revolution has created an assertive nation
that confronts us with new problems.

Underlying today's Sino-American confrontation in
power politics and Peking's vituperation against us are
certain historical sources of enmity of which we have been
largely unaware. Yet we have contributed to the impasse,
and we cannot hope to end it until we see ourselves and the
Chinese in perspective and realize the width of the gap
between us.

To be sure, China and the United States are both of
continental size and prone to consensus and self-righteousness. Each assumes that a counrty so big must be correct.

From *The New York Times Magazine*, May 22, 1966.

Each likes to think it has a message for mankind. Both remained outside the Europocentric power politics of the nineteenth century, isolated and suspicious of it, and both today find great-power status a new experience. But such similarities are far outweighed by the differences in our historical development.

The basic impediment to Sino-American understanding comes from our contrasting experiences in modern times. The expansion of Europe over the globe and the subsequent worldwide process of "modernization," in effect, created America. But at the same time and by the same means it destroyed the old China. We Americans came out of the European expansion. In our new land, we helped invent the modern world; the Chinese had it thrust upon them and rammed down their throats.

For us, the railway, for example, a century ago opened the West and built the nation. For the Chinese, with their ancient transport networks dependent upon manpower and waterways, railroads were an unnecessary foreign device used mainly by imperialist powers of the 1890s to consolidate their spheres of influence in the threatened dismemberment of the empire.

So it went with the other material aspects of modernization. Firearms, gunboats, and then a navy; kerosene lamps and then gas and electric lighting; horsecars, electric tramcars, and then buses and automobiles; modern medicine, hospitals, and public health; steam-powered factories and big industrial cities; even great social changes like the emancipation of women, beginning with the education of girls—all these things that we saw in the West as merely "new" or "modern" products of evolution and progress came to China as "foreign" (*yang,* from overseas) or "Western" (*hsi-yang*). Even the humble friction match was to China *yang-huo,* foreign fire. Thus the revolutionary changes of modern times burst into China suddenly from outside. They did not evolve gradually from within, as they did with us.

Since America arose on top of the revolution of modern times, while traditional China was caught underneath it, overwhelmed and destroyed, the American experience, opening a new continent, was exhilarating; the Chinese experience, clinging to a dying civilization, was shattering.

This contrast persists today, a subtle influence in our respective attitudes. Americans can be more relaxed about the mysteries of modern technology because they have evolved from our own past. If the modern mathematics baffles us, at least it is ours, not "theirs." Even the weird new world of space is populated by our very human astronauts, crew-cut like the boy who used to live next door. All in all, we have not really suffered in the modern revolution. Indeed, we Americans are curiously inexperienced in public suffering. Unlike most other peoples, we have never been invaded, never been defeated, never been occupied, never even been bombed.

The very word "revolution" here and in China has meanings a world apart. The American revolution of 1776 saw a change of political institutions within one part, the newer part, of an English-speaking community. The revolution's social, economic, and cultural effects were (with apologies to American historians) no more harrowing than most of American history. The Chinese revolution of 1911, in contrast, brought almost forty years of continual civil war and political frustration, but war and politics were only the smaller part of the experience. The cataclysms in economic life, the social order, thought and culture were even more dire and drastic.

Put the two experiences side by side in personal terms and one might say that the eighteenth-century Americans chilled their feet at Valley Forge, but the twentieth-century Chinese fell into a blast furnace. Take almost any yardstick of change. American youth have progressed from chaperoned dating on the front porch to going steady in the family car. Compare this with the change in China. A bride of the early 1900s went to her arranged marriage sealed inside a sedan chair and after the ceremony first raised her eyes to see what she had got for a husband, whereas today a would-be labor heroine picks out her own male co-worker to aid her in socialist production.

China's modern disaster was both caused and intensified by her having been the ancient source of East Asian civilization and the massive center of it throughout 3,000 years of well-recorded history. Two things resulted from this long development. The Chinese naturally felt superior to all the other peoples round about, and they tended to stay at home in their own vast empire. Once they had incorporated South China in the empire, they had a self-sufficient realm stretching from Siberia to the tropics. This great continental bureaucratic state lived off the farming villages and the licensed domestic trade. Overseas trade remained peripheral.

For strategic defense against the nomadic huntsmen-warriors of Mongolia, the Chinese usually tried to control Central Asia, where China's retreat or expansion on the frontiers followed the fall or rise of central power. But China from very early times was the world's largest and most populous state. It seemed to contain all things, and so the Chinese were a stay-at-home people. No one wanted to go abroad and be exiled from civilization or conquer foreign lands of lesser value. Foreigners who came were expected to bring tribute, or else they could stay away in their backwardness and obscurity.

Chinese history contains plenty of warfare, but it was mainly domestic warfare to control the empire, or on the borders to chastise the barbarians. No Chinese Alexander ever set out from the Middle Kingdom to conquer the farther reaches of the world. Chinggis (Genghis) Khan was a Mongol, and it was the Mongols, not the Chinese, who tried to conquer Japan in 1274 and 1281 and who first invaded Southeast Asia in force. After the Ming dynasty in the early 1400s had sent seven big fleets into Southeast Asia and the Indian Ocean, even across to Africa, the Chinese gave up exploration. They had the capability to discover Europe a century before the first Portuguese explorers discovered the route to China, but they were not interested in overseas expansion.

As a consequence, China's self-image today is one of victimization at the hands of a great historical and evil force invading China from the West. This makes for self-pity, resentment, and the need for an explanation of history in terms of evil and injustice.

This Western invasion is what Mao Tse-tung really means by "imperialism." Behind all the dated Leninist theorizing about economic exploitation lies the great fact of the modern world's dynamic expansion. Mao has to broaden Lenin's picture of "finance capitalism" to include the Christian missionary invasion as cultural imperialism. In the end, nearly all of China's foreign contact in modern times, the whole tragedy, turns out to have been a struggle against imperialism. The "thought of Mao Tse-tung" explains what happened to China as the victim of imperialism and tells how to beat the imperialists—who still exist —by national modernization, Maoist-style. "American imperialism" thus has an essential role in Mao's cosmology.

In defense of the American self-image, it will avail us little to argue the rights and wrongs of history with an innocent, injured "Who, me?" attitude. We are stuck with the facts: China was an ancient center of high culture, self-sufficient and isolated. The expanding West and its mod-

107

ern nations (including Japan) invaded China aggressively, undermined the old order, and left it a shambles. The Chinese culture-empire was forced to remake itself. Now that it has created a modern nationalism, its antiforeign hostility is focused on us; China's modern history is rewritten to stereotype us as evil; and there is little we can do to change it.

Since we evidently have to do the understanding for both sides, we might well begin by seeing ourselves as the heirs of the early Portuguese, Spanish, Dutch, English, and French expansionists who first invaded East Asia by sea. No one has ever been more hardy, resourceful, and aggressive than these European seafarers. Their expansion was naval, commercial, and evangelical all at once, a self-confident and formidable combination that used gunfire, greed, and spiritual conversion to undermine and break down all resistance. Native leaders were shot, bought, or converted in the first instance; only gradually could modern patriots arise to lead new nations. Small or disorganized countries became European colonies. By the mid-nineteenth century even China and Japan finally had to give the Westerners special privileges enforceable by gunboat.

This movement of Europeans abroad contributed vitally to the Enlightenment and the rise of the modern great powers. Geographic knowledge, naval technology, export industries, national rivalries, study of other cultures, the scientific view of man and society—all developed along with it. In school we learn of this vast process as the rise of modern civilization. It was what hit China.

We Americans have not liked to acknowledge all aspects of this tradition of European expansion as our own inheritance. After the Opium War we tended to agree with our envoy to China, that doughty Kentuckian Humphrey Marshall, that "Great Britain has exhibited in her Eastern conquests neither fear of heaven nor love of justice among men." Yet we, of course, demanded and got most-favored-nation privileges from China, the same as the British.

In the Chinese view of history, centuries are shorter, since there are so many more of them. The cannon of the Opium War actually boom louder in the minds of newly politicized peasants today than they did in the consciousness of China's populace at the time. Far more indignation is being voiced about it now than was expressed in 1840. And Chairman Mao's historians (like Tung Chi-ming) describe how the United States Government "early in 1842 sent a squadron as a gesture of support to the British aggressors." Actually, Commodore Kearny, suspicious of British imperialism like any good Yankee, was then seeking only to get equal opportunities for American merchants. But we got them, and now, in retrospect, we are blamed for it.

As beneficiaries—but not perpetrators—of imperialism, we claimed to be morally above it. After Dewey's victory in Manila Bay in 1898 it took us three years to suppress Aguinaldo's Philippine Republic, but to us the Philippines were always a temporary public trust, never a "colony." In our hearts we knew we were not imperialists. To an observer in Peking, however, the colonial wars of the last century in East and Southeast Asia can easily be recalled as forerunners of Vietnam today. Each modernizing colonial power had a vigorous ideological justification. Rutherford Alcock, the British consul who built Shanghai, saw trade as "the true herald of civilization . . . the human agency appointed under a Divine dispensation to work out man's emancipation from the thralldom and evils of a savage isolation." France had a *mission civilisatrice* to support and extend the blessings of Catholic Christianity. Russia felt it a sacred duty to "liberate" the oppressed peoples of the

109

Orient. By the time the Japanese generals of 1940 set out to spread "co-prosperity," they had many precedents to go by.

In theory, each expanding power wanted to let others less advanced share in the realization of its own ideals. It would be merely factual to note that our Honolulu Declaration of February 8, 1966, contains a catalogue of American ideas of peace and plenty, justice and freedom. After all, the biggest empires of the old days were built by the Western democracies, Britain and France, precisely because they were the most advanced, and therefore expansive, modern nations.

Of course, our Vietnam war today is different from the old imperialistic wars in several basic ways: We are not after territory. We support nationalist self-determination. Most important of all, we are reacting to a dynamic, Maoist political-social revolution that has an alternative program of change. The Vietcong movement in its own eyes is the latest phase of modernization, for it incorporates sentiments of nationalism, doctrines of "scientific" Marxism-Leninism, and modern technology with elements of traditional peasant rebellion. The result is something new—both a local "resistance" and a rival "imperialism" of an ideological type.

In this novel situation we feel we cannot pull out, but must try to help the South Vietnamese avoid the agonies of the Communists' meat-grinder type of social revolution. We think the Vietnamese can develop less grievously with the help of trade and aid from the international world. Yet there is little question that our mid-twentieth-century generosity is a force even more expansive, in its economic, technological, and social impact, than nineteenth-century imperialism ever was. Americans out to help you join the Great Society can be far more disruptive than the would-be imperialist exploiters of generations gone by.

All these echoes and continuities of an imperialist past that we associate with others, not with ourselves, do not make Dean Rusk a Palmerston. Nor do they invalidate, in my view, our making an unavoidable effort in Vietnam. But there is some historical resonance between our current expansion, in support of self-determination and due process in power politics, and the long-term Western seaborne expansion into Southeast and East Asia since 1500. It can give us a useful perspective on ourselves and some insight into Chinese attitudes.

All in all, the contrasting experiences of Chinese and Americans at the hands of modern history would make any Chinese patriot resentful, either at fate or at us specifically. Even if Communism had never been invented, we would probably face today a good deal of Chinese hostility. The origin of the Peking-Washington impasse cannot be blamed wholly on Marx and Lenin. Yet it is plain that Maoism cherishes a special hatred for "American imperialism."

Ideologically, Maoism explains the cosmos in systematic terms that require a heavy villain, and our "capitalism" is it. China's modern history is therefore rewritten with selected evidence to show the iniquitous propensities of American capitalists. Thus we joined in the opium trade and coolie trade, the China Coast successor to the slave trade. We collaborated with Japanese aggression when Americans "advised" Japan's expedition to Taiwan in 1874. Since American imperialism had to grow through the three stages of commercial capitalism, industrial capitalism, and finance (or monopoly) capitalism, it follows that our comparatively minor role in the opening of China a century ago does us no credit. Our aggressive imperialism was not yet fully grown. The beast had not yet got its claws and fangs.

When we did come of age in 1898, we were like bandits

arriving late at the holdup. Our Open Door policy sought two things. It demanded our cut in the exploitation of the Chinese people. It also tried to preserve their country as a unit so that we might exploit it more easily later. If one objects that our China trade was unimportant to us, Mao's pamphleteers need only quote the purple rhetoric of American expansionism from W. H. Seward to J. F. Dulles. In a China where all policy pronouncements come from authority, the fire-eating prose of retired American admirals and ex- or would-be officeholders is enough to make the flesh creep and the hair rise. The list of our aggressions becomes steadily more substantial after 1900, until we become the full-scale backers of Chiang Kai-shek's counterrevolution in the 1940s and finally the outright aggressors in Korea, Taiwan, and Vietnam. Q.E.D.

This distortion of history could be switched off at any time by Mao's totalitarian apparatus, but the hard fact is that it is logically indispensable to Maoism. Behind this lies a second hard political fact—that government in China requires a heavy stress on doctrine. The Confucian teachings of social order, with each man fulfilling his proper role, long helped a small bureaucracy to control an enormous empire.

The collapse of Confucianism and the abolition of the monarchy as a result of the 1911 revolution led to a prolonged search for a new orthodoxy. The Nationalist Government on Taiwan is still teaching in its schools the Three Principles of the People put forward by Sun Yat-sen as a new ideology in the early 1920s. Sun-Yat-senism, though less rigorous and less universal than Maoism, clearly depicts China's victimization in modern times. We must expect that any Chinese state in the present or foreseeable future would promote a doctrinaire view of history and give us our "just" deserts.

An added ingredient in Maoist anti-Americanism is its fanatic faith in the power of the human will to transform the social scene. This we can hardly ascribe to China's past. The Maoist faith in science and progress, looking forward to a future utopia, seems to be a Western contribution to China's transformation; yet it also echoes Chinese tradition —in particular, the minority rebel tradition of dynastic founders who rise from the countryside as leaders of peasant rebellion, animated by faith in a religious cult. In this spirit Mao has repeatedly pushed to meet domestic challenges by all-out efforts—fighting to defeat Chiang in the late 1940s when Stalin evidently would have waited; pressing to complete collectivization after 1953 faster than most people thought possible; finally, challenging the limits of possibility in the industrial Great Leap of 1958, which proved to be a failure. This record of extreme efforts has now been capped by Mao's challenge to Soviet Russia. One can only conclude that Mao tends to welcome an American challenge rather than Sino-American friendship.

Our relations with China are a long-term, semipermanent problem, not amenable to any quick, easy, or single solution. From our point of view, China is out of tune with the international order in which nearly all mankind, including ourselves and the Russians, participates more or less according to the rules of multistate intercourse.

Without going soft and running out, we can still meet Peking's challenge best by downgrading it. We should not accept, for instance, Chou En-lai's claim that Vietnam is a battle for the world—that the "people's war of liberation," winning there, will win everywhere. On the contrary, Vietnam is the most favorable spot for him, the least favorable for us. A stalemate will be our "victory." We should not seek more.

Second, now that we are trying again to look objectively

at our China policy we can make it plain that it is Peking, not Washington, that mainly keeps China out of the international arena. Our recent offers to permit movement back and forth of journalists, medical and public-health specialists, and scholars have been in the right direction. We should go on to permit general tourist travel, just as to the Soviet Union. Our ineffective trade embargo might as well be relaxed, on the model of our trade with the Soviets. Actually, such exchanges are likely to be held up pending Sino-American recognition, and recognition is likely to be held up pending a Taiwan "settlement," but we have everything to gain by letting it be seen that Peking, not Washington, is preventing the normalization of our relations.

The great stumbling block, for both recognition and Peking's entrance into the United Nations, is Taiwan. On this issue we can only hold to our principle of self-determination, honoring our defense treaty, keeping our fleet in the Formosa Straits, and leaving it up to the two Chinese governments in Peking and Taipei to deal directly with the UN and the world at large. Taipei is not our puppet. We cannot underwrite the ethnocentric claims of either government to rule both sides of the Straits. On this issue, too, we should relax and wait for Chinese thinking on both sides to catch up with international reality.

This effort to get the United States out of the role of free-world protagonist against Peking will not be given much help from any non-American quarter. Both our enemies and our allies seem to favor our standing forth as the container of China's revolution. But it is not in our interest to do so all alone. We should let third parties, particularly through the United Nations, participate in the arduous and long-continuing task of dealing with China. Indeed, they can bridge the gap sooner than we can.

9 HOW TO DEAL WITH

THE CHINESE REVOLUTION

The Vietnam debate reflects our intellectual unpreparedness. Crisis has arisen on the farthest frontier of public knowledge, and viewpoints diverge widely because we all lack background information. "Vietnam" was not even a label on our horizon twenty years ago. It was still "Annam" (the old Chinese term), buried within the French creation, "Indochina."

Our ignorance widens the spectrum of debate: Everyone seeks peace but some would get it by fighting more broadly, some by not fighting at all, and some by continuing a strictly limited war. Everyone wants negotiations. But to get them some would bomb North Vietnam and others would pause or stop.

Behind the cacophony of argument some hold the view that Vietnam is far away and in the Chinese realm, not in our realm. Others argue for a more global view that the balance of power and international order can be preserved only by containing the Chinese revolution as we are already doing in Korea and the Taiwan straits. Yet here the problem arises that it is not the Chinese whom we face

From *The New York Review of Books,* February 17, 1966.

in South Vietnam, but rather their model of revolution, Chairman Mao's idea. And how does one stop a revolutionary idea?

How to deal with the Chinese revolution depends on how we understand it—specifically, what is the Chinese revolutionary influence in Vietnam? And behind that, what is the nature of the Chinese revolution itself? Can we ultimately deal with it in any way short of war? But where would war get us?

A long view is needed, a historical framework within which to see all the actors, including ourselves. (What are we doing so far from home?) Yet our knowledge of East Asian history is so meager it can mislead us. "History" is used as a grab bag from which each advocate pulls out a lesson to prove his point. Some recall Manchuria in 1931: we failed to stop Japan's aggression and it led on to Pearl Harbor. Others recall our drive to the Yalu in 1950: we ignored China's vital interest in her frontier and got ourselves into a bigger war. Again, what was the lesson of Dien Bien Phu in 1954—were the French strategically overextended or merely tactically deficient in airpower?

"History never repeats itself" means that one can never find a perfect one-to-one correspondence between two situations. Each must be viewed within the long flow of events, not as an isolated lesson. The Vietnamese and Chinese have had their own specific ways and interests, traditions and attitudes, and their own East Asian pattern of contact, not in the Western style.

China's revolutionary influence on Vietnam comes from a long past. In the first place, Vietnam grew up as part of Chinese culture—the East Asian realm which included not only China in the center but also the peripheral states of Korea, Vietnam, and Japan. All these countries took over the Chinese writing system in ancient times and with it the

Chinese classical teachings, the bureaucratic system of government, and the family-based social order. These countries have an ancient common bond in philosophy, government, and cultural values.

In Vietnam's case, this Chinese heritage was imposed by a thousand years of Chinese rule in North Vietnam, the ancient homeland of the Vietnamese before they expanded southward into the Mekong delta. Independence from Chinese rule was gained by fighting in the tenth century A.D., but Vietnam then continued for another thousand years to be "independent" only within the Chinese realm and tribute system. Down to the 1880s, Vietnamese tribute missions going over the long post route to Peking, acknowledged the superior size and power, the superior culture and wisdom, of the Chinese empire and its rulers. This filial or younger-brother relationship was broken only a few times when Chinese armies again invaded Hanoi (for example, in 1406 and 1789), only to be thrown out by the Vietnamese resistance, whereupon tributary relations were resumed. There were only these alternatives, to be ruled by China or to be tributary, in the Chinese cultural-political-psychological sense, taking China as a model. This went to the point of using the same structure of government and copying the Chinese law codes verbatim, with the same terminology, in Chinese characters, which were the official writing system.

Vietnam's growth in the shadow of China was eventually balanced by the arrival of sea invaders from the West. The early Portuguese adventurers and later Dutch and British East India Companies landed their ships at Danang (Tourane), where our marines are today. This sea contact with the expanding West climaxed in the French takeover of the 1860s and '70s. French colonialism during its eighty years brought both exploitation and moderni-

117

zation, in a mixture that is hotly debated and can hardly be unscrambled.

We Americans have thus had predecessors (even the Japanese in 1940–1945) on the long thin coast of Vietnam. We are sleeping in the same bed the French slept in, even though we dream very different dreams.

Western sea power in Southeast Asia goes back 450 years. Europeans expanded westward into the empty Americas very slowly. They went east into populous Asia more quickly and easily. The resulting colonialism in Southeast Asia has now been superseded by the new relationships we are trying to work out in the name of national self-determination. We are on an old cultural frontier between the international trading world and Asia's land-based empires. Vietnam, like Korea, has been caught in the middle and pulled in two.

Vietnamese patriots reacted against the French by learning modern nationalism from them. In so doing they continued to be influenced by the Chinese example to the north. The Chinese reformers of 1898 had their counterparts in Hanoi. Sun Yat-sen operated from there in 1907–08. When his Chinese Kuomintang reorganized itself on Soviet lines in the 1920s, a Vietnamese Kuomintang followed suit. In the same era, the Chinese Communist Party set a model for the growth of a Vietnamese Communist movement in the 1930s. The rise of Ho Chi-minh illustrates this trend. Both the French and Soviet Communist movements and Chiang Kai-shek's Whampoa Military Academy were in his background.

By the time the Chinese Communists came to power in 1949, they were in an even better position to give the Vietnamese the encouragement of example. Viet Minh patriots of the united front were trained to fight against the French in the sanctuary of South China. When the People's

Republic of North Vietnam eventually emerged in 1954 after the defeat of France, it was indebted to Chinese help but, most of all, to the Chinese Communist example.

Today in South Vietnam, the "people's war of liberation" has developed from the Maoist model that took shape in China during the struggle against the Nationalists and the Japanese. Mao's formula is to take power through a centralized Leninist party that claims to represent the people. This begins with establishing a territorial base or "liberated area," inaccessible and defensible. From this base, the party organizers can recruit idealists and patriots in the villages and create an indoctrinated secret organization. Once under way, this organization can begin to use sabotage and terrorism to destroy the government's position in the villages and mobilize the population for guerrilla warfare. Shooting down unpopular landlords or government administrators has a wide demonstration effect. When guerrilla warfare has reached a certain level, it can escalate to fielding regular armies, strangling the cities, and completing the takeover.

One appeal of this Maoist model is its do-it-yourself quality. The organizing procedure is carried out by local people with only a minimum influx of trained returnees and essential arms. The whole technique cannot be understood apart from the local revolutionary ardor that inspires the movement.

In China today we confront a revolution still at full tide, an effort to remake the society by remaking its people. Chairman Mao spreads a mystique that man can overcome any obstacle, that the human spirit can triumph over material situations. For seventeen years with unremitting intensity the people have been exhorted to have faith in the Chinese Communist Party and the ideas of Mao Tse-tung. With this has gone a doctrinaire righteousness that has

119

beaten down all dissent and claimed with utmost self-confidence to know the "laws of history."

Mao's revolution puts great stress on the principle of struggle. The class struggle has made history. Each individual must struggle against his own bourgeois nature. China must struggle against Khrushchevian revisionism. The whole world must struggle against imperialism led by the United States.

Out of all this struggle among the 700 million Chinese has come a totalitarian state manipulated largely by suasion. Individuals work upon themselves in the process of thought reform, criticizing their own attitudes. Residential groups maintain surveillance on one another, as children do on their parents, as part of their national duty. Terror is kept in the background. Conformity through a manipulated "voluntarism" fills the foreground. No such enormous mass of people has ever been so organized. The spirit of the organization continues to be highly militant.

The sources of China's revolutionary militancy are plain enough in Chinese history. The Chinese Communist regime is only the latest phase in a process of decline and fall followed by rebirth and reassertion of national power. In this revival, many elements from the past have been given new life—the tradition of leadership by an elite who are guardians of a true teaching, the idea of China as a model for others to emulate.

Because the Chinese empire had kept its foreign relations in the guise of tribute down to the late nineteenth century, China has had little experience in dealing with equal allies or with a concert of equal powers and plural sovereignties. Chairman Mao could look up to Comrade Stalin. He could only look down on Comrade Khrushchev. An equal relationship has little precedent in Chinese experience.

The most remarkable thing about China's political history is the early maturity of the sociopolitical order. The ancient Chinese government became more sophisticated, at an earlier date, than any regime in the West. Principles and methods worked out before the time of Christ held the Chinese empire together down to the twentieth century. The fact that this imperial system eventually grew out of date in comparison with the modern West should not obscure its earlier maturity. Thus the ancient Chinese had a chance to concentrate on the problem of social order, staying in the same place and working it out over the centuries. Even before the Chinese unification of 221 B.C., ancient administrators had worked out the basic principles of bureaucratic government. They selected for their ability a professional group of paid officials who were given over-all responsibility in fixed areas, instructed and supervised through official correspondence, and rotated in office. The Chinese empire thus very early embodied the essentials of bureaucracy which the Europeans arrived at only in modern times.

As the Chinese sociopolitical order matured and grew, its influence radiated outward over the Chinese culture area. Because China was the center of civilization in East Asia, it served as the model for smaller states like Korea and Vietnam, whose rulers naturally became subordinate to the Chinese emperor. This hierarchic relationship was expressed in the tribute system already noted. But the rise of nomadic warriors like the Mongols on the grasslands of Inner Asia posed a new problem, for they were non-Chinese in culture and yet their military capacity enabled them to invade North China and eventually conquer the whole empire. The result was another Chinese political invention, under which it became possible for powerful non-Chinese peoples to participate in Chinese political life.

This they did either as allies and subordinates of strong Chinese rulers or, in case of Chinese weakness, as the actual rulers of China itself. Thus the ancient Chinese empire again showed its political sophistication. Invaders who could not be defeated were admitted to the power structure. The Mongols in the thirteenth century and the Manchus in the seventeenth century could even seize the imperial power, but they had no alternative to ruling China in the old Chinese fashion.

When Westerners arrived on China's borders in early modern times, they also began to participate in the Chinese power structure. They were generally given status as tributaries and until 1840 were kept under control on the frontier. Thereafter, the Westerners had to be allowed to participate in the government of China. This they did with special privileges in treaty ports protected by their gunboats and under their own consuls' extraterritorial jurisdiction. In its beginning, this nineteenth-century treaty system followed Chinese tradition.

Eventually, of course, Western contact brought in new ideas that undermined the old Chinese order. But not all the new ideas of modern times were wholly accepted. China picked and chose what it wanted to accept from the West. Scientific technology and nationalism were in time taken as foundations of economic and political change. But Western-style republicanism and the election process did not take hold.

Even a brief sketch of the historical experience of the Chinese people indicates their cultural differences from the West. Some of these inherited differences have been selected and reinforced by the new totalitarian rulers. Chinese tradition is, of course, very broad. It affords examples of a Confucian type of individualism and defiance of state control. Some day these examples may be invoked for democratic purposes, but that time has not yet come.

Today we see these cultural differences affecting the status of the Chinese individual. The old idea of hierarchic order persits. Enemies of the new order, as defined by it, are classed as not belonging to the people and so are of lowest status. On the other hand, party members form a new elite, and one man is still at the top of the pyramid. The tradition of government supremacy and domination by the official class still keeps ordinary people in their place.

The law, for example, is still an administrative tool used in the interest of the State; it does not protect the individual. This reflects the common-sense argument that the interest of the whole outweighs that of any part or person, and so the individual has no established doctrine of rights to fall back upon. As in the old days, the letter of the law remains uncertain and its application arbitrary. The defense of the accused is not assured, the judiciary is not independent, confession is expected, and litigation is frowned upon as a way of resolving conflicts. Compared with American society, the law plays a very minor role.

The differences between Chinese and American values and institutions stand out most sharply in the standards for personal conduct. The term for individualism in Chinese (*ko-jen chu-i*) is a modern phrase invented for a foreign idea, using characters that suggest each-for-himself, a chaotic selfishness rather than a high ideal. Individualism is thus held in as little esteem as it was under the Confucian order. The difference is that where young people were formerly dominated by their families, who for example arranged their marriages, now they have largely given up a primary loyalty to family and substituted a loyalty to the party or "the people." In both cases, the highest ideal is sacrifice for the collective good. Similarly, the modern term for freedom (*tzu-yu*) is a modern combination of characters suggesting a spontaneous or willful lack of discipline, very close to license and quite contrary to the Chinese ideal of disciplined cooperation.

The cultural gap is shown also by the Chinese attitude toward philanthropy. Giving things to others is of course highly valued where specific relations call for it, as when the individual contributes to the collective welfare of family, clan, or community. But the Christian virtue of philanthropy in the abstract, giving to others as a general duty, quite impersonally, runs into a different complex of ideas. Between individuals there should be reciprocity in a balanced relationship. To receive without giving in return puts one at a serious disadvantage: one is unable to hold up one's side of the relationship and therefore loses self-respect. American philanthropy thus hurts Chinese pride. It has strings of conscience attached to it. The Communist spurning of foreign aid and touting of self-sufficiency fits the traditional sense of values. American aid does not.

Cultural differences emerge equally in the area of politics. In the Chinese tradition, government is by persons who command obedience by the example they set of right conduct. When in power, an emperor or a ruling party has a monopoly of leadership which is justified by its performance, particularly by the wisdom of its policies. No abstract distinction is made between the person in power and his policies. Dissent that attacks policies is felt to be an attack on the policy maker. The Western concept of disputing a power holder's policies while remaining loyal to his institutional status is not intelligible to the Chinese. Critics are seen as enemies, for they discredit those in power and tear down the prestige by which their power is partially maintained. (This idea also crops up in Taiwan.)

Another difference emerges over the idea of self-determination. This commonplace of Western political thinking sanctions the demand of a definable group in a certain area, providing they can work it out, to achieve an independent state by common consent among themselves. This idea runs counter to the traditional idea of the Chinese realm that embraces all who are culturally Chinese within a single entity. Thus the rival Chinese regimes today are at one in regarding Taiwan as part of the mainland. Both want to control both areas. Similarly, they are agreed that Tibet is part of the Chinese realm without regard for self-determination. A supervised plebiscite would seem so humiliating that no Chinese regime would permit it.

Both Chinese party dictatorships of modern times are also believers in elitism and opponents of the election process, except as a minor device for confirming local popular acquiescence in the regime. Elections on the mainland are manipulated by the party. Taiwan has developed a genuine election process at the local level, but the old idea of party tutelage is far from dead at the top. Here again, a case can be made for the Chinese practice. Our point is merely its difference from that of the West.

Perhaps the most strikingly different political device is that of mutual responsibility, the arrangement whereby a designated group is held responsible in all its members for the conduct of each. This idea goes far back in Chinese history as a device for controlling populous villages. At first five-household groups and later ten-household groups were designated by the officials, ten such lower groups forming a unit at a higher level, with the process repeated until a thousand households formed a single group. In operation this system means that one member of a household is held accountable for the acts of all other members, one household for the acts of its neighbors, and so on up the line. This motivates mutual surveillance and reciprocal control, with neighbor spying on neighbor and children informing on parents. Communist China uses this ancient device today in its street committees and other groups. It directly denies the Western idea of judging a man by his intentions and condemning him only for his own acts.

Cultural differences lay the powder train for international conflict. China and America can see each other as "backward" and "evil," deserving destruction. We need to objectify such differences, see our own values in perspective, and understand if not accept the values of others. Understanding an opponent's values also helps us to deal with him. The old Chinese saying is, "If you know yourself and know your enemy, in a hundred battles you will win a hundred times."

All this applies to our present dilemma in Vietnam where our military helicopter technology is attempting to smash the Maoist model of "peoples' war." We face a dilemma: appeasement may only encourage the militancy of our opponents; yet vigorous resistance may pose a challenge that increases their militancy. Fighting tends to escalate.

One line of approach, quite aside from military effort, should seek to undermine the militancy of our opponents. Why not pay more attention to their motivation and try to manipulate it? Having seen how Mao Tse-tung has manipulated Khrushchev and Chiang Kai-shek has manipulated us, can we not do some manipulating ourselves? There are several elements to use. One is China's enormous national pride, the feeling in Peking that this largest and oldest of countries naturally deserves a top position in the world. The Chinese attitude of cultural superiority is deep-rooted and still plays a part in foreign contacts.

A second element is the need of any Chinese regime for prestige. Peking rules an incredibly vast mass of people by means of an enormous and far-flung bureaucracy. The prestige of the leadership and the morale of the populace and bureaucracy are intertwined. The rulers must seek by all means to bolster their public image, show themselves successful, and make good their claims to wisdom and influence. For seventeen years Peking has buttressed its prestige by attacking American imperialism, but its need for prestige is more basic than any particular target of attack. Are there other ways to strengthen itself than by denouncing and "struggling against" the biggest overseas power?

Another element is the converse of the above—the accumulated fatigue of revolution. Chairman Mao's exhortations to continued struggle and austerity betray his lively fear that the new generation will grow tired of permanent revolution. His eventual successors may respond differently to opportunities abroad. Finally, there are the concrete problems of the Chinese state, its need for foreign capital goods and food supplies, needs that may grow.

A program to take advantage of these elements, recognizing the realities of cultural difference, would seek to enlarge Peking's international contact and work out a greater role and responsibility for China's rulers in the world outside. Many express this in wishful terms—"If only China would join the international world." Realists point out Peking's reiterated refusal to do so on any feasible terms. What I am advocating here is not a single gesture but a continuing program, not an alternative to present policies but an addition to them. It is too simple to say that one cannot oppose an avowed enemy on one front while also making an accommodation with him on other fronts. On the contrary, this is what diplomacy is all about. The whole idea of manipulation is to use both pressure and persuasion, both toughness and reasonableness, stick and carrot, with an objective calculation of the opponent's

127

motives and needs. This is not foreign to President Johnson's thinking.

On the issue of Communist China's entry into the United Nations, one objection is that Peking in repeated declarations has set impossible terms. Peking demands that "America get out of Taiwan" and that the Nationalist government leave the United Nations entirely if the Peking government enters any part of it. These are terms we cannot accept. They are thus tough bargaining positions. But we should never expect Peking's entry into the United Nations to be achieved by a single cataclysmic act. It can only follow a long and tortuous negotiation, probably involving the whole organization. Negotiations of a sort are already under way.

The most practical objection to Peking in the United Nations is the trouble it will cause. The Communist capacity for impeding orderly procedures, obstructing and sabotaging collective effort, is well known. The prospect of getting mainland China into the international organization is not one to gladden the heart of any official who must deal with the resulting situation. No one should assume that our China problem will be easier. The argument for getting Peking in is simply one of choice between evils. The trouble it brings will be less grievous than the warfare that seems likely if Sino-American relations remain on their present tracks. We have learned to prefer small limited wars to big nuclear disasters. So we should try to substitute diplomatic wrangling and nasty competition with China all across the board in place of a prolonged military showdown.

In short, Peking's presence in the United Nations is no panacea; nor is it likely to seem to be a great improvement. It may at first seem like a disaster, and this has deterred every administration in Washington. But the presence of

China in the United Nations offers a prospect of diversifying the struggle and diverting it from the military single track. Can we afford to let the Chinese revolution remain in its partly imposed, partly chosen isolation, hoping it will eventually lose its militancy?

We can do much more to deal with the Chinese revolution than merely shoot at its protagonists to contain it militarily. The need for disarmament and for worldwide cooperation over population and food supply are only two of the forces pushing us toward a more active China policy.

What conclusion emerges from a survey of China's revolutionary history and the cultural differences that separate us?

First, we are up against a dynamic opponent whose strident anti-Americanism will not soon die away. It comes from China's long background of feeling superior to all outsiders and expecting a supreme position in the world, which we seem to thwart. Second, we have little alternative but to stand up to Peking's grandiose demands. Yet a containment policy which is only military, and nothing more, can mousetrap us into war with China. Our present fighting to frustrate the Maoist model in Vietnam is a stopgap, not a long-term policy. We should add to this policy and, if possible, substitute for it a more sophisticated diplomatic program to undermine China's militancy by getting her more involved in formal international contact of all kinds and on every level.

The point of this is psychological: Peking is, to say the least, maladjusted, rebellious against the whole outer world, Russia as well as America. We are Peking's principal enemy because we happen now to be the biggest outside power trying to foster world stability. But do we have to play Mao's game? Must we carry the whole burden

129

of resisting Peking's pretensions? Why not let others in on the job?

A Communist China seated in the United Nations could no longer pose as a martyr excluded by American imperialism. She would have to deal with United Nations members on concrete issues, playing politics in addition to attempting subversion (which sometimes backfires). She would have to face the self-interest of other countries and learn to act as a full member of international society for the first time in history. This is the only way for China to grow up and eventually accept restraints on her revolutionary ardor.

10 THE IMPACT OF

PROTESTANT MISSIONS

The divergence between the American people and the Chinese Communist Party is nowhere more evident than in the interpretation of China's modern history and the role Christian missions played in it. Chairman Mao's slogan of "politics in command" means that history like all intellectual activity should be a tool of the regime in its effort to remake China and its people. Nearly all Western contact in modern times is thus relegated to the status of imperialist aggression, and within this framework missionary activities become cultural imperialism.

On the other side of the Pacific, the American account of mission work in China is still mainly an internal and subjective one, recording the efforts made in the missionary movement, who participated when and where, and the concrete results achieved. Little attempt has yet been made to explore the impact of Christian missions on China's transformation—their external influence on the whole society, including side effects and repercussions not purposed by the missionaries. Thus Kenneth Scott Latourette expressly noted in 1928 that his great pioneer survey was *A*

From *Christianity and Crisis*, June 27, 1966.

History of Christian Missions in China and not a history of the Christian *Church* there.

Historians of China since 1800 are concerned with the whole spectrum of change: how the traditional Confucian order gradually collapsed, partly in response to Western contact, and how the new nationalistic order slowly emerged, reflecting in part the ongoing processes of Chinese history. Missionary activity is here viewed from the outside, as part of the "Western impact" that produced cultural conflict and social change, the spread of education and technology and the transformation of values. The missionary's interaction with the society as a representative of Western culture makes him an integral part of the Western expansion. Similarly, in the Chinese view of modern history, the expansion of Christianity is seen as part of the expansion of Europe, and both are now regarded as aggressive.

The xenophobic view now current in Peking will be strengthened as the record of culture conflict is further studied. It will then appear that the Protestant missionary movement actually helped to undermine and destroy the leadership of the Confucian scholar-official class. This nineteenth-century culture conflict was muted at the time because the participants were each confined within their own cultures, talking to their own constituencies and seldom communicating across the cultural gap. The missionary and the Confucian gentry had little language in common. Only today is there, on either side, a historical perspective on the nineteenth century that is mutually communicable and intelligible, even if not agreed upon.

The contemporary Peking propagandist-historian can allege the following points that, with rather slight modifications, will probably receive general acceptance.

The Confucian scholar-official ruling class and the Western Protestant missionaries had different views of the world, beginning with different evaluations of the individual's place in society and the function of his religion in his social life. This was a basic conflict of values.

Missionaries studied the Chinese language mainly as a tool for the propagation of their faith. While some became founders of Sinology and led the way in educating the West about China, the majority remained profoundly culture-bound and devoted to the original cause that had brought them to China. Toward Chinese religion and custom they were generally unsympathetic and often aggressively iconoclastic. Likewise, the Confucian scholars as a class retained their original beliefs and values and continued to regard Christianity with aversion, until they gradually died out as a social group. The number of Christian converts from the scholar class before 1900 was quite small.

The conflict of economic interests between China and the West was less obvious than that in the religious sphere. Western merchants, on the whole, found reliable opposite numbers among Chinese merchants. They shared a common profit motive. Far from being competitors in exporting Chinese produce abroad or importing Western products, they needed each other. The long-term effect of foreign trade may or may not be regarded an injurious, but the contact of foreign and Chinese merchants was on the whole friendly and cooperative. In contrast, the contact of missionary and Confucian scholar was very slight and usually avoided by the latter. There was no common enterprise, except in matters of immediate urgency like famine relief or certain scientific endeavors. As bearers of antithetic ideologies, the two groups were competitors and usually enemies.

The general effect of Protestant teaching and example was to set up an alternative to the traditional Confucian order. In the Protestant dispensation, the individual had a greater degree of personal freedom from his family and community obligations. Through the priority given to his faith, he was absolved from loyalty to his ancestors and other social superiors as his first duty. This directly conflicted with the Confucian teaching of social order that maintained a superior-inferior status between the sexes and the generations. Implicit in the background were the legal conceptions on both sides. Doctrines of individualism were directly at variance with doctrines of collectivism; concepts of natural and civil rights clashed with concepts of hierarchic order and duties to superiors.

This conflict was made more intense because the missionaries were expansive. Indeed, they were militantly aggressive even in their own thinking and terminology, because this seemed essential if they were to make any progress at all on the vast Chinese scene. Thus Protestantism "invaded" China to achieve a "conquest." After 1866, the China Inland Mission sought to reach every part of the interior. Missionaries were not invited in; they came of themselves.

As foreign nationals in China, the missionaries were covered by the provisions of the treaties, in particular by extraterritoriality under the legal jurisdiction of their national consuls. They could not get rid of this privileged status no matter how they felt about it. In order to defend the foreign position in general, the consul had to help the missionary claim his special legal status. If a missionary were attacked or his property damaged, the consul, in his own national interest, could not let the matter go unnoticed. The treaty system meant that missionaries were representatives of their home countries, even when they felt themselves to be least connected with their own governments.

As a result the diplomats had to back up missionary demands for protection, residence, and property owning. The missionary invasion thus had behind it the full force of the foreign powers. This was most obvious in the case of the French support of Roman Catholic missions. As Edmund S. Wehrle shows in his *Britain, China and the Antimissionary Riots, 1891–1900,* the British government in the 1890s tried to control all British missionaries and prevent their getting into situations that might produce conflict. Yet because of England's own principles of free enterprise, such control could not be really established or enforced. On the other hand, interests of state demanded that, whether controlled or not, the missionaries when attacked must be defended.

These general points can probably be accepted to a considerable degree by historians both in China and abroad. But they represent only one aspect of the long process of collapse of the old order and building of a modern nation. The vogue in Peking now is to stress the negative and deleterious effect of the Western impact, including missions, and to attribute China's progress to unaided efforts by the Chinese people to fight back against foreign imperialism. The basic assistance rendered by missionaries in constructing a new China is perhaps the main part of the Christian story there, but this is of no interest to Peking and has been pretty well lost to view. It does not fit the Marxist-Maoist book.

This means that the task of rounding out the story must be performed by Western historians. It is precisely here that cooperation between the missionary establishment and the academic historical researcher is most needed. The contribution of Protestantism to the rise of modern China is extensive and ubiquitous. The record is to be found in missionary archives and elsewhere, but thus far it has hardly been adumbrated.

The following points will probably emerge as research proceeds. They form the positive part of what would otherwise remain a negative story.

The confrontation with an alien culture led missionaries from the beginning to study Chinese and to take the lead in the development of modern Sinology. Elijah Coleman Bridgman at Canton for example, began language study in order to spread the Gospel. But very soon he and S. Wells Williams, his missionary printer, founded the *Chinese Repository,* which for twenty years (1832–1851) provided a stimulus for the Western examination of Chinese culture and learning. From this generation emerged James Legge and his monumental translations of the classics, achieved with the help of gifted assistants like Wang T'ao.

The early arrivals quite soon saw the value of medical missions as an adjunct to proselytism. Dispensaries and hospitals pioneered the development of China's modern medicine. The Medical Missionary Association was formed as early as 1887.

Missionary education, inaugurated for the training of an indigenous pastorate, soon faced the problem of including English in its curriculum and admitting students not solely interested in religious training. Teachers in these schools organized the Educational Association of China in 1890. The progression by which the early schools became the Christian colleges of the twentieth century was steady and significant, and of great influence in the nation's modernization.

As China's problems worsened in the late nineteenth century, a whole wing of the missionary movement began to take an interest in the amelioration of living conditions.

Pioneers like Timothy Richard, who led the way in famine relief in the 1870s, represented the growing social concern of a whole generation. It was evident that the country needed technology from the West, as well as evangelism, to alleviate material conditions that would otherwise hold back the spirit indefinitely. Out of the social gospel came an interest in the reform movement of the nineties. The role played by Timothy Richard, Young J. Allen, Gilbert Reid, and others as inspirers or precursors of the reform movement is now recognized, for example, in a recent study by Wang Shu-huai of the Modern History Institute of Academia Sinica at Taipei, entitled "Foreigners and the 1898 Reform Movement" (*Wai-jen yu wu-hsu pien-fa*). In this era missionary writings at last began to reach the scholar class, who now had to face China's defeat by Japan and the imminent breakup of the empire.

The movement also inspired an approach to the problems of urban youth through the growth and spread of the YMCA and YWCA. This energetic program in major cities and universities performed in its day the task of organizing educated youth for personal and social betterment.

Finally, the increasing role of Christian converts on the Chinese scene after 1901 represented an achievement of the Church that still remains to be assessed in social terms. A whole generation of reformers was raised up. Many became leaders in the remaking of China. The fact that the Western and Christian model of leadership stressed personal and community development, rather than the building of state power, meant that in the end this group would not become dominant. Yet their contribution was obviously enormous.

Underlying all those forms of missionary influence was a guiding Christian concept of individualism. This inspired, for example, the attack on footbinding and the emancipation of women from illiteracy and child marriage. By the negative example of his privileged presence, the missionary no doubt aroused Chinese nationalism. But by his positive efforts he encouraged individualism.

No historical work is likely to do justice to this entire subject. To leave it unstudied, however, will create a distorted view of what happened in modern China. A valuable chapter in the cultural history of Sino-Western relations will also be missing. There is thus every reason for a concerted effort to promote historical studies both of the missions and of the Chinese Christian community.

11 REFLECTIONS ON

"THE CHINA PROBLEM"

Cultural differences between China and America compli-
cate their power relations by building up the threat that
each seems to pose for the other. Mao sees American imperialism as China's deadly enemy. On our part we well
may wonder whether the American vision of individual
rights and personal welfare may not meet its main opponent in China. One hopes not, but the evidence thus
far available does not promise otherwise.

The China problem is only beginning to mushroom
above our horizon. Twenty years hence it may fill the
Western sky. Armageddon may not ensue. But any realist
will calculate the chances of disaster in the effort to
avoid it.

First of all we have to accept what the Soviets acknowledge, with perhaps greater realism than ourselves, as the
"coexistence (competition without nuclear war) of great
powers with differing social systems." In other words,
Chinese Communist totalitarianism is going to be with us
for a long while, and we are going to have to live with it
and learn to deal with it. Even if China should miracu-

From *Diplomat*, September 1966.

lously cease to be Communist, it would still have to be totalitarian; state and community would still dominate the individual. "The freedom of the individual" cannot be expected to develop there, in our American sense of the term. No doubt we can accept this if the Chinese people can do so; we cannot undertake to liberate them.

But what if the Maoist model of revolution is widely exported and taken up among the peoples of underdeveloped countries? For a nation of missionary-reformers, who see American ideals gaining ground at home, this will be hard to accept abroad. We recognize that peoples undergoing a population explosion, in the midst of the modern revolutions of nationalism, economic growth, and social change, are likely to prefer strong government to civil liberties. They cannot as yet afford our political living standard. More peoples than we expect may buy Chairman Mao's package of disciplined party, indoctrinated army, and village bases under ideological dictatorship. Our China problem was excluded from public discussion for more than a decade because it became too upsetting, too "controversial" and distasteful; yet to face it in the future may require even more perspective than we needed in 1950.

Part of our perspective must be a fresh, Fulbrightian look into ourselves. We may well be a people of infinite potentiality, but in fact, we are mainly devoted to the doctrines of individualism and the practice of commercialism. Certainly the two go together, for the modern corporation flourishes as a juridical individual, protected by its legal rights, while it maximizes profits by catering to the average consumer, manipulating his individual hopes and fears. Our great society is to be built by meeting the small wants of you and me. Our vast domestic problems are formulated in terms of educating individuals, keeping them healthy, unpolluted, and employed, transporting them between home and work, integrating them in the community, easing their old age. Our government, we say, exists to serve such purposes. Our foreign policy, even when most expansive—if not, indeed, aggressive—aims to give other peoples a chance to develop in a pluralistic world of individual nations that may join in international trade and cultural exchange. Meanwhile, our largely commercial distribution of goods, services, mass media, and technology, blankets much of the earth.

In China both individualism and commercialism have been, and are still, highly disesteemed. This is one thread of continuity between ancient China and the present day. Confucius propagated a social order in which he was esteemed most who subordinated best. Filial piety stood for a secular religion. It carried over into ancestor reverence. Social harmony and personal welfare depended on it.

Individualism of our type had no place in the old Chinese social order for a number of reasons. Each individual depended upon his family-clan for his status, livelihood, education, and even recreation. China's religions did not stress personal immortality. China's legal system developed no doctrine of natural rights or of the supremacy of law to protect such rights. China experienced neither a renaissance nor a romantic movement. It has remained a crowded land, whose people live close to nature and are dependent on production by muscle power, with little surplus for high living standards. It still has a moral code favoring personal austerity and collective effort. Self-limitation is nobler than self-realization.

Similarly, commerce in the old China never got free of official exactions. In the classical teachings, trade was considered sordidly materialistic and unproductive. Traders regularly had to pay for official protection to ward off the depredations of other officials. Unlike the Calvinists, Puritans, and other forebears of Western entrepreneurship, Chinese merchants developed no moral sanction for the worth and inviolability of profit-oriented activity.

Against this background, Chairman Mao has had little trouble reversing the modern Chinese efforts toward American-type individualism and commercialism. Exponents of liberalism, like Dr. Hu Shih, could find no support in the law, nor an independent judiciary capable of defending civil liberties. The Shanghai bankers and merchants who arose in the shadow of Western extraterritoriality could never break free from Chinese officialdom.

This difference in values between Chinese and Americans makes it easy for each to regard the other as essentially immoral. Our great power rivalry can be superheated by the moral righteousness that is second nature to both peoples. Surely an immoral enemy is an evil thing deserving destruction. To Chinese youth who are exhorted to save the nation by postponing marriage to the ages of twenty-six and thirty, the current American vogue of sexual liberty may well seem undisciplined, licentious, and depraved. To a whole people on short rations, trying to industrialize on a rice-and-bamboo living standard, American levels of commercially induced consumption and wastage must seem at least irresponsible, possibly perverse and in any case undeserved.

On our side, the suppression of dissent in China will continue to seem a threat to our values. Enforced confessions, the contrived voluntarism by which intellectuals offer to immolate themselves in manual drudgery down on the farm, the spurious enthusiasm of mass demonstrations on demand—all the manipulations of China's national collectivism will seem to us the opposite of freedom. "People's wars of liberation," with their indoctrinated idealism and calculated terrorism, are only one of the menaces emanating from such a society. But when peasant lads of the People's Liberation Army storm our guns like a human sea, we must realize they are neither stupid dupes nor hopped-up fanatics. They merely believe in self-sacrifice, of a sort that our code of individualism hardly comprehends. All in all, to say the future is fraught with danger of Sino-American conflict seems to be putting it mildly.

Yet the future is not foreclosed, and Americans may develop the insight and self-control to deal with and contain the Chinese revolution, in the proper sense of the term. The overburdened word "containment" should mean resistance to aggression, not to the expansion of all Chinese influence. Containment is only half a policy. It tries to negate the use of force and subversion against other peoples, but it requires the holding out of feasible alternatives to aggression, and it must be balanced and accompanied by programs of peaceful intercourse, by noncontainment. Dulles' prescription of military containment and economic-diplomatic isolation was a recipe for producing an eventual explosion. A growing number of Americans now recognize that containment of any Chinese aggression must be balanced by encouragement of China's peaceful participation in the international world of diplomacy, trade, travel, information, disarmament negotiations, and technical and cultural exchange. This balance cannot be soon achieved, but at least the idea has been accepted that military containment must be accompanied by constructive contact.

If Sino-American relations gradually become a two-way street, our impact on China (which was far more upsetting than Americans ever realized) must eventually be balanced by some Chinese impact on America.

We have already seen this retroaction in the case of

Japan. "Opening" of her own accord after Commodore Perry's black ships entered Edo Bay in 1853, Japan became a modern nation with amazing speed. Today, 113 years after Perry, the new Japan is our major trading partner.

This Japanese example raises a disturbing question. Must the sequence of Japan's modernization, expansion, defeat, and eventual friendship with us be repeated with China, but on a larger scale? Or can we by a great effort cut into the unhappy syndrome of great-power conflict and avoid a further phase of violence? American air attacks close to the Chinese border of North Vietnam may have triggered the answer before these words are in print. If not, we must still prepare for years of Sino-American hostility. In one way or another we shall have to respond to the competition of Chairman Mao's model of revolution.

One admonition that emerges from all this is the supreme need of *balance* in our response to Maoism, not only between determination and flexibility—a balance of judgment—but also between our military and nonmilitary efforts—a balance of operations.

We are too easily led astray by our own institutions, in particular by the status and function of the military in American life. We are proud that our armed services have a properly subordinate status and a limited technical function in our nonmilitarized society. But for these very reasons our armed forces are in no position to deal alone with an across-the-board, political-social-economic total struggle like the Maoist model of revolution. Admittedly, civil action in a war-torn country like Vietnam must be led by the local government and people. But the American temperament is to separate wartime from peacetime, give the military mission all-out priority, and achieve the feats of logistics and firepower that we best know how to achieve. The result may be military success, a basic imbalance in

144

the total effort, and possibly an over-all failure. Our single-minded military effort may wreck an economy through inflation, corrupt merchants and officials, antagonize patriots, and disintegrate a society rather than mobilize it for nation building. We can do better, but only by mobilizing our own effort on a more-than-military basis and keeping all the parts moving together.

Toward China a balance of containment and contact—informational, commercial, cultural, and diplomatic—may take years to achieve. But one will avail little without the other.